FINDING YOUR WORTH IN THE MIDDLE OF A BROKEN HEART

VALENTINA RICHARDSON

authorHOUSE

AuthorHouse™
1663 Liberty Drive
Bloomington, IN 47403
www.authorhouse.com
Phone: 1 (800) 839-8640

© 2020 Valentina Richardson. All rights reserved.

No part of this book may be reproduced, stored in a retrieval system, or transmitted by any means without the written permission of the author.

Published by AuthorHouse 12/21/2019

Scripture quotations marked NIV are taken from the Holy Bible, New International Version®. NIV®. Copyright © 1973, 1978, 1984 by International Bible Society. Used by permission of Zondervan. All rights reserved. [Biblica]

ISBN: 978-1-7283-3858-3 (sc)
ISBN: 978-1-7283-3859-0 (e)

Print information available on the last page.

Any people depicted in stock imagery provided by Getty Images are models, and such images are being used for illustrative purposes only.
Certain stock imagery © Getty Images.

This book is printed on acid-free paper.

Because of the dynamic nature of the Internet, any web addresses or links contained in this book may have changed since publication and may no longer be valid. The views expressed in this work are solely those of the author and do not necessarily reflect the views of the publisher, and the publisher hereby disclaims any responsibility for them.

This book is dedicated to the man that broke my heart for the last time and to the men that I allowed to break my heart over and over again.... thank you for bringing me to Gods throne. Also to the women that think this earthly love from a man can heal you... please know that you're not alone! Trust God and he will heal all the wounds!

Intro

It was rainy and cold outside as my grandmother and I walked to the house that I was sleeping at. You see I was 6 years old and didn't have a home; my mother wasn't living in her own place and my grandmother got ill and needed surgery so she lost her job and apartment. My aunt was a senior in High School and was working overtime to save enough money to help my grandmother get back into her own place. In the meantime, I was staying with a family friend. The family that I was staying with were kind to me but it still wasn't my family. I always looked forward to the weekends because that meant I got to be with my grandmother and aunt. My grandmother would pick me up every Friday and take me to the movies, out to eat or broadstreet (a part of the town with shopping stores). I always had a good time with my grandmother she made me feel special and sacrificed a lot for me. On Sundays I dreaded having to leave her just because I enjoyed her company. As she would walk me to the house I was staying at; I would always get sad and think to myself "why can't I have a regular family, living in a regular house, with two parents and no drinking, smoking or domestic violence." As a child you should not have to feel like a lost puppy with no home, no parents and no bed to call your own. As my grandmother dropped me off, she would walk me upstairs and waited till I showered. She would then read me a bedtime story until I fell "asleep"; well I would act like I was "sleeping" because I didn't like my grandmother walking home in the dark. Once I heard her leave, I would cry myself to sleep wishing for a home where I can be with my family. This was the first time I can say I discovered what abandonment, despair or loneliness felt like. Little did I know that I would become an expert on the feelings of abandonment, boundaries being crossed, betrayal, rejection, loneliness, deceit, pain, disappointment and let down from my parents and many other people in my life. It all started when I was a child and because of the dysfunction that lingered until I was in my 30's. Unfortunately, the dysfunction was all I knew; the dysfunction was my normal atmosphere. As a kid growing up, I didn't know how to conquer the dysfunction. It was so powerful because I allowed the dysfunction and hurt to rule my inner and outer being. I did not see anything but dysfunction so how would I know that I was going down a wrong road. I stood a victim to my upbringing which was in my past and allowed my behavior to wreak havoc on my spirit. The last heartbreak was my wake-up call to every unhealthy characteristic I had developed and all the toxic behavior I have allowed to live within my circle. I decided to allow God to take over. After 25 years of hiding my illness that slept within and tormented me daily; I put down my mask and allowed God in. Throughout my years of dysfunction, I learned the art of escaping the thoughts of my inner pain. I always ran away from hurtful situations or painful memories. The first time I ran away was when I joined the military. Joining the military was a way of escape and starting a new life for me. I would be away from my family that I felt was so different than I, the heartbreak of my child hood love; because he was having a baby and my abortion that I refused to admit. I didn't like who I was and definitely didn't want to stay in the streets of New Jersey. I would soon use the military in every way to help me escape my pain through constantly moving. After 13 years of moving and hiding in the military it obviously didn't work for me. I had more baggage after the 13 years of service than when I was a child; I fell head over heels in love with men that had a phobia for committed relationships. I also learned that I would settle and marry men that I wasn't truly committed to. The irony in that?! As I walked away from the military; on paper; I was an accomplished 33 year old woman heading back to Jersey to intern at SIRUS XM RADIO and work nights and weekends on-air in south jersey. I decided to go back to jersey and start this super fun new career; I would go to school for radio and T.V. broadcasting. This new career would be me yet again running away from my purpose and calling that God created me for; too bad I just didn't recognize it. My days on the radio was an experience I would not take back but I recognized in those days that I was missing something deep inside; I didn't know what it was. It was a Sunday afternoon and I was on-air on "Ocean Counties only hit music station" and I felt empty, lost, alone, distracted, not fulfilling my purpose and I said to God what do I do now? He said is this what you want to do for the rest of your life and not have an impact on anyone's life? Do you not want to save souls and help those in need? Do you just want to do meaningless gigs on air that only benefits your ego? Do you want to live a life with no significant meaning? Please be mindful when I say "God Said" I mean that small inner voice that lives inside of each of us but we ignore it or just don't tap into it. In that moment in the middle of commercial breaks I sat there and thought to myself... I cannot do this for the rest of my life! This is not my calling. That day I sent an email and gave my two weeks' notice. I decided that I would help people and apply for the Masters Program in Texas and become a Counselor. In this moment I decided to step into the unknown and finally lean on my faith to do what God has called me to do. That meant giving up my security blanket and pursuing a career I knew nothing of but it also meant that I would help people but the reality is I wanted to help myself too. The whirlwind of the next 6 years would bring unimaginable loss. Not in three life times could my brain fathom what happened in this time frame. The shock of my brother physically dying along with my grandmother and emotional deaths of relationships which could be interpreted as a season of loss; but for me God showed me that the loss created resiliency inside of me that was needed for my purpose.

This book is meant for the little girls that had no typical family with the picket white fence or the women that have loved so hard that they lost their worth in the process. Throughout these pages you will learn about grace beyond gratitude, humility, strength beyond measure, forgiveness without boundaries, peace without calamity, true joy in the midst of the storms....but this is when my eyes were opened to the beauty that lied in my ashes. Get ready to become a new version of yourself that you never knew existed! Much love and smiles, Mrs. Richardson ♥

CONTENTS

Chapter 1   Abandonement 1

♥

Chapter 2   No Voice 9

♥

Chapter 3   Boundaries 17

♥

Chapter 4   Celibacy 23

♥

Chapter 5   Date Yourself 31

♥

Chapter 6   Submission 43

♥

Chapter 7   Rejection 49

♥

Chapter 8   Intimacy 59

♥

One

ABANDONEMENT

"For my father and my mother have forsaken me, But the LORD will take me up" Psalm 27:10-14 New International Version (NIV)

I WAS BORN AND RAISED in Newark, N.J. in the summer of 1980 to a feisty firecracker family. The town was located in a middle to low class neighborhood mainly filled with minorities. The streets were made up of Puerto Ricans, Dominicans, African Americans, Haitians, Cubans, Colombians and Portuguese people. All these nationalities made up the mixture of cultures that surrounded me. These cultures instilled in me characteristics of courage, honesty, quick tempered, wisdom and accepting of all races. The East Coast especially in the upper tristate area of New Jersey is filled with corner stores called "Bodegas". In these "Bodegas" the cheapest 5 cent bubble gums, now a laters, sugar daddys (the sugar cane chewy candy), poppers gum, lollipops, toilet paper, vegetables, sazon, cigarettes etc. was sold. This was a one stop shop for anything my family would need for the house or if the kids wanted junk food. On any given day a bombox could be playing salsa, merengue or hip hop with the older men or women sitting on delivery milk crates. Usually these old men or women would be gossiping about all the drama of the block or they would be playing cards, dominoes or dice. In my town we had the best salsa nightclubs and Portuguese restaurants. A lot of the New Yorkers would come to New Jersey to enjoy the night scene simply because they could get more party, drugs or liquor for their buck. Now my family wasn't made out of money but they sure knew how to have a good time and make everyone in their presence laugh. Our financial status didn't rob me from developing good memories but it did sometimes put me in more than one place to call my home. Newark is the town I grew up in but as for my mother and father they had a different upbringing. My mother was originally from New York City. She was raised by a single mother and her great grandmother in NYC until she was 12 and then my grandmother moved to New Jersey. You see my mom grew up with a mother that had strict rules and demanded that you respected her rules and if not; you would quickly get reprimanded. Her mother did not play; she would quickly discipline with a shoe or her heavy hand across her face if anyone was to disrespect her. She also wasn't afraid to speak her mind at any time. If you were to ask my mother how was her childhood, she would say that the spirit of abandonment and distress loomed in her home. The definition of abandonment I'm referring to is as follows: "To relinquish, renounce; mean to give up all concern in something. Abandon also means to discontinue any further interest in something because of discouragement." (Mariam-Websters Online Dictionary; 1996) Very interesting to read that some of the causes of abandonment is no interest because of feelings of discouragement. You see my grandmother felt discouraged in regards to her parenting skills and her role as a mother. Since she wasn't emotionally fulfilled or had a role model to mimic with her own children; she had a heavy spirit of discouragement. These feelings led my grandmother to display abandonment to my mother which provoked my mom to feel that her upbringing was hell on earth. She felt her mother was unavailable, she wasn't reasonable and didn't favor her much. It's now that my mother states that she was indeed loved by her mother but in the only way she knew how and that was by tough love. My nana wasn't raised by a present or loving mother; she was raised by a single mother that did not show love in the traditional sense.

My mother was the oldest of four girls born to parents that did not communicate or even know how to function in a marriage. My grandparent's marriage was filled with domestic violence, neglect and disrespect. In turn; they were not loving or understanding parents themselves to their daughters. Due to the lack of complete and whole parents; my mother was sent to be raised by three main family members; her great grandmother, grandmother and Uncle David. From the age of twelve and on my mother didn't have her father; you see my grandmother left my grandfather and moved to New Jersey to start a new and safer life for her two children. During this time there was not a positive male role model except for my grandmother's brother Uncle David. The yearning for a male role model was growing in my mothers' heart; little did she know that this was a need that started since she was a young girl. Her father was "present" but his love was not; even though he was in her "presence". Once my grandmother was established in New Jersey she sent for her daughters but soon after; my mother was acting out in disobedience and my grandmother sent her to live with her Uncle David. After a year of living with her Uncle my mother asked to go back to her mother's house because of the many rules that her Uncle David instilled in his home. He was a retired Marine and had time to nurture, conversate and enjoy his niece but my mom felt restricted and missed her mom. You see in my nana's house she had more freedom to do whatever she wanted and at times she could be disrespectful. This is only because my nana was a teacher and owned a restaurant at the time and wasn't home much because she had to maintain the family business. As my mother got older, she married the first man that could get her out from under my grandmother's roof. Little did my mother know that the same roof she was desperately trying to get up out of she would be pleading to come back to. After a short year; my mother's husband started to occasionally put his hands on my mother as she would do the same to him. The same domestic violence that my nana went through; my mother endured as a child. Unfortunately, she also endured as an adult in her own marriage. This is when the generational cycles continued and the new dysfunctional family behavioral patterns began for my mother at the age of 17. This is when abuse became the norm and my mother started to emotionally disconnect from love and would look at men as the enemy; definitely not as a significant being that she should be submissive too. My grandmother quickly sensed that my mom was getting abused by her husband and threatened him with a knife and addressed his beatings to my mom. Soon after my mother left her husband and moved back with my grandmother; my mother filed for divorce. One thing about my grandmother is that she always had her family's back no matter the current dysfunction within her own relationship with her family members. I want to explain the depths of the dysfunction that developed in my grandmother's childhood that she carried into her adult life with her own immediate family. The English definition of dysfunction reads as follows: abnormal or unhealthy interpersonal behavior or interaction within a group. (Marriam-Webster's Online Dictionary; 1996) The behaviors that my grandmother witnessed as a child were not normal or healthy; the behaviors created dysfunction in my grandmother's mental wave of thinking and a deterrence in her emotional developmental aspects of her brain. My grandmother was raised in the dysfunction of violence, alcohol abuse, drug abuse, abandonment, lack of affection or emotional disconnection. My grandmother was born in NYC to a mother and father that had a volatile relationship that ended quite abruptly, and my grandmother didn't spend much time with her biological Dad after he left, he was from Spain and wasn't much of a father role model. She also had an older brother "Uncle David" he was opposite of my grandmother. He had blonde hair and fair skin; his father was Cuban and also was not present in their lives. Soon after my grandmothers biological father left; my grandmother's mom was extremely violent and abused my grandmother. Unfortunately, the negative characteristics of my great-grandmother transcended to my nana and this was her norm. This was her life; she was raised in a home with no father and a mother that abused her children either mentally and emotionally by pawning them off to be raised by their grandparents. My grandmother was always dropped off at her grandmother's home because of the dysfunction of her mom. My grandmother was taught to be independent, courageous, vocal, street smart and never to fear a man! Her mind interpreted those characteristics to become a woman on the outside that portrayed strength, intelligence, dominating personality and in power of all her emotions but in reality; she was that 9 year old girl that was vulnerable and abandoned. She was left to her grandmother to raise; alone. As she became an adult, she did not feel the need for a man to fulfill her accomplishments. So, in turn my grandmother didn't know how to show love to a man and never-mind to her own daughters especially not in a way that would make them feel appreciated, loved and respected. It's important to notice the generational patterns that started three generations before me and understand that knowing how to receive love from a man or to be submissive was not a normal concept to me or any of my family members. On the contrary my grandmother did believe that in order to leave her grandmother's house quickly she would need to marry…soon. This is when she met my grandfather and they both quickly married and had daughters. My grandfather was Puerto Rican and did not show one ounce of love for his wife. Now they tried to love but would fight each other along the way. My mother was dropped off at her great grandmother's house to be raised as her mother and father would hit all the nightclubs and become friends with people like Ceila Cruz, Hector Lavoe and Tito Puente. From the outside looking in; it looked like my grandparents were living the life of the rich and famous. A typical night for them was to walk into a club, get VIP treatment by the manager paving the way for them to the front of the club and personally bringing out a table directly in front of the stage and moving others out of their view. It was no big deal for them to enjoy a night of dance and laughter then a nighttime of disrespect and domestic violence. It was then my grandmother began to imitate the same negative behavior that her mother did when she was a child. As you can see all of the behaviors of my great-grandmother, grandmother and mother all shared the following common characteristics: abandonment, emotional neglect, physical abuse and disconnected parents.

As my mother grew older her and my grandmother would hit the nightclub scene together since they both enjoyed Latin music. Now it was in one of these popular Colombian nightclubs that my mother and father met in the summer of 1978. They were only together approximately 4 years and on May 28, 1982 my mom comes home to find that my father took off to Texas without telling her! Mind you it was her BIRTHDAY! You see after my Dad was gone about a year my mom chose to surprise him and unbeknown to her he already moved on with his High School sweetheart; so she chose to come back to Jersey. The first memory I have of my dad I was about 8 yrs. old and he came to visit me and took my whole family out to eat because my aunt wouldn't allow him to take me on his own; she was afraid he would take me back to Texas. My aunt was the head of the family even though she was the youngest. She took the responsibility of providing for the whole family; mind you it was just my grandmother, mom and me but she was only 16 yrs old. My mom couldn't find a good paying job that would allow her to live in her own place and take care of a toddler so this is when my aunt became the head of the household because my mom had to move in with her baby sister and mother.

Now, I was raised with opinionated strong women but no male role models and I didn't realize that this was a problem until I became a teenager and my aunt Marie and uncle Todd separated. My father was unavailable because he was incarcerated soon after his trip to see me when I was 8 yrs. old. He got involved in illegal drugs and weapons. That lifestyle and greed of money didn't take too long before the Feds busted my father. While my father went to trial and got sentenced to 25 years in prison; my heart was in shock. I truly didn't know how to feel besides a heavy spirit of abandonment as I grew up without a father. Little did I know that as my father was in prison; God was stepping in and becoming my only father that I will ever need.

I learned how to compartmentalize the pain I endured for the yearning of my Dad and I was forced to be ok. No one asked me about my feelings about my Dad being incarcerated. I felt that there was not one person I could connect with. I chose to embark on the male role model I did have and that was my Uncle Todd. During my father's incarceration; I had two significant role models in my life; my Uncle Todd during my adolescent years and my Uncle Amaro from 15 till today. My Uncle Todd was the only man that portrayed a positive influence in my adolescence years. He made sure to check in with me emotionally and intellectually. He showed me the essence of a man complimenting his girlfriend and providing for his family. I remember the first day I met him; I was seven years old sitting in my kitchen and my aunt came home with him to introduce him to our family. I was so excited to meet another human being and the fact that he was a male I felt an overwhelming amount of gratification. Todd being around made my family become more conscience about family dinners. My Uncle Todd always included me and sometimes he would make my aunt and me travel to different places that I never was taken before. I felt safe while he was in the house. There was a different perspective that was expressed during our family conversations. The most significant memory that Todd left with me was the essence of the C.D. player and Michael Jackson. He bought me my first C.D. player and C.D. it was the Dangerous album by Michael Jackson. That was our thang we would listen to music and watch videos and he would explain to me the origin of the music and the culture of the music. Every Friday Uncle Todd would take me and my childhood love Mr. Italian to McDonalds. Mr. Italian was a family friend that was always included to any function Uncle Todd was involved in. He would take us to McDonalds and I would order a number 2; 2 cheeseburgers, French Fries and a caramel ice cream with nuts on the bottom and top. On the weekends he would take us shopping or to the movies. I always looked forward to the weekends because uncle Todd would purposely spend time with us and introduced us to new hip hop songs. Mr. Italian was a joy to grow up with and I always would want him around because our families were similar. Little did I know that Mr. Italian would be the first young boy and man I would fall in "teenage love" with. I'll explain later. During my young adult years; Uncle Todd actually introduced me to my favorite rapper of all time L.L. Cool J. We always went to the City to look at the new restaurants or events they had going on. Until the age of 15 my Uncle Todd was my barometer on what to look for in young men and when none seem to match up, I would entertain whatever came close. You see during the years of my personality forming and my brain developing my likes and dislikes is when Uncle Todd was in my life. My aunt and him broke up right before my 15th birthday and I was as devasted as If my father and mother were separating. I started hyperventilating and experienced a panic attack. Todd had to calm me down and that's the first time I felt heartbreak from a male. In my mind it was me he didn't want to no longer be around and I definitely knew in my heart I would never have that bond with him again; even though he reassured me that our bond would never change; it did! I want to be clear and say I understand that I was not Todd's responsibility and I can see how it would be out of place for him to be constant in my life. My aunt moved on and Todd's presence would be a bit disrespectful to my Uncle Amaro. Soon after my Uncle Amaro came into my life; my eyes were opened to a new world of hip hop music, clothes and learning how to write rhymes. My uncle Amaro taught me how to D.J. on real turn tables, he taught me how to behave as an artist and he taught me patience! My Uncle Amaro is my go to guy to talk about anything and everything Hip Hop, world events, conspiracies and celebrities. His spirit is a calming but contagious energy that I yearned for then and grateful for now. My uncle taught me to never be ashamed of my roots or my unique abilities in life. He gave me my radio on air name and pushed me to dream a dream bigger than my last one. Needless to say, he's the man I admire today! He is selfless, loving, humble and courageous. His soul is as deep as the ocean but his love is as wide as the earth and I thank God for him! I am grateful for the men God did assign to me in my childhood and will forever be grateful to their contribution to my being today.

Even though I had a mother, grandmother, aunt and uncle (s) that geared me in my life; I still found myself feeling abandoned and yearning for a level of unconditional love.

Knowledge Nugget:

My Power is more than where I was raised; my experiences is where My POWER derives from. It was the BREAKING of my SPIRIT and LIFE that produced my drive to be more than where I came from!

Two

NO VOICE

"For all have sinned and fall short of the Glory of God"
Romans 3:23 New International Version (NIV)

As a teenager in High School I was the girl that got along with everybody; like a chameleon I easily blended with any type of students. I enjoyed my High School years; I had tons of friends, good teachers and excelled in all my electives now my academics…is another story. Of course, in High School there were tons of young boys that were appealing but only one caught my attention. I was attracted to the sneaky Mr. Quiet; you see he was my type: Tall, Caramel Complexion, Perfect Teeth, Muscles and dressed like a pure breed east coast dude. I noticed him because he was in my cooking class and every 6th period I would admire his face and desperately seek his attention. I was a freshman and he was a sophomore but I didn't care. I knew what I wanted and my type and so I went for him. He was very quiet in class but I noticed he would look at me a lot so one day one of my good friends approached him about me and gave him my number. As time went on, we ended up talking in class then after class but it wasn't because he called me or came up to me NO! I did all of the work...now Ladies, read closely. I DID ALL THE WORK! He did not call me, think of me, contact me or introduce me to his friends. It was in this moment I should've stood up and voiced my wants and needs as a young lady in this non-committed relationship with him. I should've acknowledged my inner desires and wrote them down then proceeded to tell him and if he did not want to adhere to my desires or listened to me that's when I should've went along my way. Did I? NO! I chose to spend time with him and when we were together or even talked on the phone it was me going to his house, going to his classes or calling him. Honestly, looking back at that little girl that was barely 15 with no idea on how a young lady should be courted. I had no married couples to compare how relationships should work and I yearned for a male's attention. I followed my heart; if I missed him, I believed I should call him and if I wanted to see him, I believed I should go and see him. I didn't realize that when a man wants you in his world, he will hunt you down and properly love you into being his woman. I was young and lost with no sense of respect or value for my presence in a man's life. As a young lady my focal point should've been my studies and my talents that God gave me; not running after a young man! After my first year with Mr. Quiet I started to discover that he was unfaithful, lying and not interested in me so I "broke" up with him even though he wasn't committed to me but I chose to not call or seek him. During this time, I quickly jumped into another relationship; yet again Ladies!!! This is what we do wrong, instead of taking time to invest into ourselves or our education we choose to invest into another man! I started a new job and loved all the attention I was receiving from Mr. Gentleman; he was not my type but was emotionally and physically available. He was a little older than me, a hard worker and owned his own car. He was kind to me, listened to me, bought me gifts, took me on dates, interreacted with my friends, provided for me and made me feel safe! I didn't love him like I did love Mr. Quiet; I cared about him and appreciated him but no love lived there for him. I would later... about 25 years later realize that he was an actual blessing to me but I was too blind by the super cute but unavailable ex-boyfriend to realize. During the year of dating Mr. Gentleman, I experienced happiness and resentment that I would carry with me for 25 years. I lost my virginity to Mr. Gentleman and became pregnant! I'll never forget the moment I found out I was pregnant; it was about two weeks of my stomach not doing well and constant vomiting. Since I was a sick child; I believed that I had a virus so I asked my mother to take me to the hospital. As she was gathering her things; I quickly thought to myself "WHAT IF I'M PREGNANT" so I quickly grabbed a pregnancy test that my aunt had hidden in the closet and took it. Those 5 minutes were the longest in my life! As I sat on the toilet seat and waited and waited; my life flashed before my eyes "how could I be pregnant at 16, while I'm in High School"! I thought to myself there's no way my family could take care of another living soul they barely could afford me and my two siblings. I basically had a nervous breakdown while waiting for the test results. As soon as the 5 minutes were up and my mom is yelling outside the bathroom for her to take me to the hospital; I check the test and sure enough I'M PREGNANT! I quickly gathered myself together and told my mom I felt better and I didn't need to go to the hospital. Soon after she left, my grandmother looked at me and said "Your Pregnant" I looked at her and said yes. She said figure it out; I then called Mr. Gentleman and told him the news he quickly said whatever you want to do I will be by your side. I told him I have to get an abortion and he said are you sure? I said yes... I have to... there's no way I can have a kid. He said ok, I'll figure it out. In that moment I should've spoke up and voiced my thoughts and concerns of getting an abortion; I should've used my voice and asked my counselor in school for information in regards to the procedures of an abortion. I should've confided in my best friend to go with me to Planned Parenthood and asked them information on abortion. But I didn't! I kept my mouth shut and went along with what I was told to do. If I only knew I would live with this guilt and resentment for 25 years. It's a shame that I didn't have support or guidance on what exactly abortion does to the pea size embryo. The precious life that lives in an embryo that God decided to bless me with I had it sucked out of me and went about my life as if I did not end an innocent soul that lived inside of me. Of course, I would regret my abortion for years on end when I couldn't get pregnant and actually never had a kid by the age of 35 as I planned. But in that 16-year-old girls brain I had no choice; my grandmother wasn't supporting me and I had no idea how to raise a child. She was only doing what she knew was right and I don't blame her at all! Better yet I didn't have the courage to take on this new challenge and rely on God to carry me through. I didn't even know that God!! Definitely not the God that is my father today.

The moment I received my abortion I became disconnected with Mr. Gentleman and stopped talking to him. He kept calling me and trying to see me but I could not bring myself to see my act of sin. I wanted to never see him and never look back upon my huge mistake so I moved on with my life as if nothing ever happened. I only told my best friend and grandmother about my abortion. I felt like a horrible person inside and tried to hide what I did by overcompensating every child I ever met from then on. I emerged myself into my favorite electives and found another job. Eventually, Mr. Quiet swarmed himself back into my life and all the infidelities came back with him. Our relationship was on and off again and on and off again for 4 years. During one of the "OFF TIMES" of Mr. Quiet and I, Mr. Italian ended up coming back into my life but not from a family function. One of my best friends knew how much I adored Mr. Italian during our adolescent years so she secretly set up a double date with him and I. I was so shocked to see him pull up to the driveway to take me out. My heart was screaming with joy! As we went to the pool hall and stayed out until the late night, we exchanged numbers and became the two young best friends we once were. We went out, watched movies and had deep conversations on life and love. I was finally enjoying my childhood crush and I couldn't believe it! Ladies! Of course, I was the one falling in love and he was just enjoying an old friend and us reminiscing on the good ole days. So you can understand how deeply I cared for Mr. Italian and how drastically I committed to men who did not show half of the effort or commitment I had to them. My friends were going on a couple's trip to Jamaica and I wanted Mr. Italian to go with me so I asked him and he said yes. I was sooo happy but why wouldn't he go I was PAYING for it!!! Ladies! Why in the world should I be paying for a grown man to go on a trip with me. Mind you... we had no commitment to each other and we were not labeled as girlfriend and boyfriend. I was so desperate it was pathetic! But I was working doubles and making that money to pay 2,000 dollars for a couple's trip to Jamaica and I was excited! REALLY! Anyway, the time came to go on this trip to Jamaica and Mr. Italian was NO WHERE TO BE FOUND! I was freaking out! I went to his house and stood outside waiting to see if I saw him! NOTHING! He was not answering my calls or beeper notifications (yes, that's how long ago it was; we had beepers)! I was so heartbroken! But why would I believe that this man that made no effort, commitment or sacrifice for this trip; would show up! I decided to call his sister since her and my aunt were best friends. She stated that he was in jail, he got put in jail the day before and there's no way he would be going to Jamaica! I was beside myself! I was flabbergasted! Now I had to figure out who's going to go with me! I'm grateful that in the last month Mr. Quiet was eagerly trying to get back in my good graces so I decided I'm going to ask him. Sure enough in 24 hours Mr. Quiet re-arranged his work schedule and he came with me. We became ON AGAIN after our trip to Jamaica but that didn't last long. Mr. Italian ended up contacting me a year after the Jamaica trip apologizing but we never were the same. I went back with Mr. Quiet just because I couldn't deal with the pain of rejection from Mr. Italian. It wasn't long before until I realized I couldn't live in settling for Mr. Quiet! I told Mr. Quiet I was done! I was scared because he was the only form of love that I was receiving. After I broke up with him for good, I decided to join the military, I felt liberated because I was starting a new life in the military. I wanted to leave my childhood love Mr. Italian and his new girlfriend and new baby behind me. The day he revealed to me that he was having a baby just shook my inner being and I knew joining the military was the right thing to do. No more of Mr. Quiet's lies and deception or Mr. Italian's perfect family in front of my face and I definitely wanted to leave the dysfunction that was present in my own family. I would have a new start into a world I had no idea about but I knew it was time.

My beautiful cousin joined the United States Air Force and one day when she came home on leave, she convinced me that it was the best thing I could do is join the Air Force and, in that moment, I realized that would be my ticket to a new life and a new beginning! I did just that; I went to her recruiter and joined the Air Force! It was the best decision I have ever made. Basic Training for the US Air Force is in San Antonio, Texas. I wasn't a fan of Texas; this is where my father's family lived and I didn't like it much. I would visit Texas when I was younger and wasn't impressed! Even though I wasn't fond of Texas I sure was excited to be in San Antonio and start this new career in the military. No one in my immediate family was in the military and I was determined that I would make it through successfully. The two months at Basic Training were the most challenging obstacles physically, mentally and emotionally but I made it and I had new techniques, skills and mindset for this country and for my future and I was ready to take the world of the military. Soon after I joined; 9/11 happened and I was thrown into the worldwind of terrorist information exercises and long nights of manning the office but I was ready and grateful! I grew a sense of love for America and the American People; I found my purpose. This jersey girl was helping the military get the bad guys; I was helping people that actually made a difference in this world. My eyes become wide opened to a world that is bigger than Newark, New Jersey and I was loving every moment of it. I decided then; that I would be the best Airman that I could be by putting Integrity First, Excellence in all I do and Service before Self. After the war on terrorism calmed down a little, I started to ask my Chief if I could go back to the basic training squadrons on Lackland Air Force Base and brief them on the Initial Enlistment Bonus and how it worked since that's one of the programs my office handled. I wanted them to be financially literate and I was determined to help them be the best young airman they could be. It was during this time of me going to the Training Squadrons that I met Mr. East Coast. I always yearned for an educated and positive role model and as I got older, I would be attracted to men that are tall, educated, an east coast swag with a personality that commanded your attention. The first time I saw Mr. East Coast I was intrigued at his height, body structure, accent and his versatile knowledge of the Hispanic culture. I also admired the fact that he was a Military Training Instructor; to me that was an elite position and I was impressed. He was recently divorced and extremely helpful to me because at the time I didn't have a car. He loaned me one of his cars so I wouldn't have to walk on base to work in the Texas heat. Now looking back, I realized that him loaning me his car was a way "In". I was so young about 22 and I didn't think he was using his car to draw me closer to him but it worked. I was impressed that he was very generous with his time, money and compliments. You see I was raised in a home where if a man spends money on you and buys you gifts; then he's definitely worth your time. In my mind the more money and gifts a man would spend on me then the more he loved me. That idea of love is so far-fetched; I was basing love off of material items instead of true sacrifice. It's shameful to say but that's what I saw growing up; if a man loves you he will buy you jewelry, food, clothes, perfume or give you money to get your nails done. This is so trivial because a man that is courting you and wanting to make you his wife will be paying off car loans, student loans, mortgages or pouring into your future business. Now that's a sacrifice! Growing up I was shown and told continually by my family that a man needs to buy you items and spend money on you. Yet again it's because of the dysfunction, poverty and abandonment that they experienced so their mindset was a poverty-stricken mindset. When I say poverty stricken mindset I mean a mindset that constantly tells them their in need or will be in need. So the behavior that lines up with this frame of thinking is take take and take some more just in case I won't have or just in case the man leaves. As long as the man is spending money then he's making a sacrifice in their eyes. You see my great grandmother, grandmother and mother had a poverty mindset; meaning: we may not have anything to eat tomorrow so take everything you can now while you can. The reality is... society today; shows young females that love equals money. I carried and lived by this motto until the age of 37. Society doesn't teach us that the essence of love is dying to self everyday; in order to show your spouse your selflessness. The more time I spent with Mr. East Coast I fell in love with him or what I believed was love. In my mind; he met my needs: he paid for my food CHECK he took me out CHECK he provided a means of transportation CHECK... that was it. Then as time went on, I started to feel unappreciated and disrespected. There was this one incident that I will never forget; it was a Friday night and I went to his house to spend the weekend and he had his best friend visiting from New York which was a female....need I say more. Well, I will, so you get the full picture of this fiasco; I walked into his house and she was sitting and acting very comfortable as if she lived in his house. As he began to introduce me to her; the energy that she gave me and her disrespectful attitude was beyond acknowledgement. I ignored her demeanor and continued to act polite and respectful. I started a conversation with her since she was from the east coast like me and a female; I figured we could connect on that level but her attitude was dismissive and cocky. I started to notice she was making side jokes about me to her other little friend and my boyfriend was laughing along. I felt so undervalued and embarrassed so I decided to go upstairs to bed. About 15 min. later my boyfriend came upstairs and told me get up I'm taking you home. I was like oh ok I'm out. Inside; my heart was hurt, crushed, devastated but silence filled the whole car ride home while his bff was sitting in the front seat. In that moment I should have spoke my mind and stood up for myself but I just stood quiet. Yet again, I should've used my voice and stood up for myself and his wrong doings but I chose to not stick up for myself. My fear was; I didn't want him to choose to never see me again. Now how ridiculous does that statement sound! He needed to worry about me not seeing him anymore for his actions towards me while his bff was talking behind my back. He should've stood up for me and represented me as his queen. He didn't and I was worried. The fact of the matter is that I didn't have a voice and definitely didn't establish firm standards. I yearned for a man's presence more than having my value to be respected. I allowed disrespectful behavior towards me just to be in the presence of a man that showed me some attention. Soon after I was dropped off; Mr. East Coast called me apologizing and wanting to see me so of course I agreed. Our relationship lasted about a year and he broke up with me. In that moment I lost myself so I did what I always did… I ran away! I volunteered to go overseas and I got what I wanted. I was chosen to do a tour in Germany. This is where my God will meet me at my point of need … one on one!

Knowledge Nugget:

Our mistakes don't limit us only our fears do!! Overcome the past and soar into your FUTURE! You are an OVERCOMER! ACT LIKE IT!

Three

BOUNDARIES

Scripture: "A day for the building of your walls! In that day the boundary shall be extended" Micah 7:11 New International Version (NIV)

ONCE I GOT THE ORDERS in my hand to go to another country, I was a ray of emotions: scared, excited, motivated, eager, grateful and ready to see the world. I was 24 years old when I got on the military aircraft to fly to Germany and once I arrived my supervisor and my squadron met me at 1145 pm with open arms. I felt the true essence of wingmen when they welcomed this young airman. The Air Force Base in Germany is located in Western Europe and is a family-oriented base. This is where I met ladies that would bring me to the feet of Jesus and change my spiritual life forever. The dorms where I lived was surrounded by Christians; I learned about Joyce Meyer, I became born again and baptized on this base. I learned about praying and believing in God and his son Jesus Christ who died for me. I attended my first women's retreat and this is when I released all the guilt, I felt for having an abortion. Even though I felt alone on this base far away from the U.S.; my soul and spirit were getting put together. I attended church, bible study and personal bible study as well. I was learning so much about my father and what the definition of a Christian was. I was on fire for Jesus! After about 7 months of working in the Employments office which meant I was responsible for gathering all the records of the incoming personnel. One day as I was getting ready for the new batch of personnel coming in I would look at the names of the records that I gathered and I would tell my boss which ones I wanted to in process; as they got off the plane. I wanted to get first dibs on how they looked before they hit the base. So, as I'm going through my weekly folders and reviewing the names, I see a different but authentic name. I say to myself…hmm… this name seems like it belongs to an interesting fella. I tell my boss hey I want to do the next plane that comes in cause I think I wanna check out this one dude. He always laughed at me and would play along with my shannanigans. As the plane arrived there, I was looking my best; as much as a female could in a green battle dress uniform but I had my lashes popping, my eyeshadow gleaming and my teeth shinning with my big smile. The moment the new inbound airmen lined up I knew exactly which one was Mr. Intelligent; I could tell with his demeanor and once his eyes met mine oh I knew. I'm in!

As he walked up to me to inprocess I looked at him and said Welcome to Germany with my big smile and anxious heart eagerly awaiting to be loved and claimed. He smoothly smiled as well and turned in his information. A couple of weeks passed by and I would see him around the base; we also had mutual friends so he was introduced to me a couple of different times. You have to understand how the base was; it was a tight community of military members and family that stood close to each other. Basically, you can go anywhere on base and at least every 3rd person shared something in common with me. The base had a burger king, subway, bowling alley and a small chapel. I lived in the dorms on base and Mr. Intelligent lived off base; soon after we officially met and hung out at the Enlisted Club we automatically just hung out day after day. Instead of me setting boundaries and informing him of my standards; instead I allowed him to cross over into my personal space, living space and mental space. Keep in mind LADIES! I take full responsibility for the lack of strength I didn't have to outwardly proclaim my boundaries.

This is where we go wrong; we must always set boundaries in our lives with friends and especially with men that we are intimate with. Since no boundaries were set and no official courting went on between us and no official dates where he asked for my permission to be my boyfriend. It was just the two of us hanging out, making out and going out to the movies then I claimed myself as his girlfriend. Soon after he moved into my dorm room and we became an item; everyone on base knew we were an item but no conversation was had between the two of us… LADIES!! That's the problem; we assume the role as a girlfriend when the dude is just happy because he doesn't have to go alone to the E-Club or movie theatre and I'm being committed, obligated and attentive. I jumped the gun too fast instead of taking the time and not sleeping with Mr. Intelligent and just getting to know him and his background but how could I get to know a man when I didn't even know myself! As we become adults and start to become mature ladies we must write down our boundaries and be specific with the items we write down. Then we must put pink or yellow stickies with the boundaries in our bathroom, dashboard in the car and on our keyboard at work. We need to constantly be reminded of what our boundaries are so when the devil sends a counterfeit into our life that seems like he had all the standards you wrote down but only missing a few from your list; you can identify the fraudulence in the man aka distraction the devil sent. Since I did not have the wisdom I have today; I allowed Mr. Intelligent to get deeper into my soul and I found myself getting ready to marry him. Yep I was 24 and ready to be married because my self-inflicted checklist said by the age of 25 I had to be married and have 2 kids and well I just turned 24 and I'm late! Why do we create unrealistic pressures in our minds because society paints a picture in movies about where and how we should live? If society would paint the right picture that we the women on this earth should first dig deep inside our own intelligence and roots before we involve ourselves with men in a not so much committed relationship! Early on in our relationship my bladder started to act up and the Urologist diagnosed me with a bladder condition called interstitial cystitis basically painful bladder syndrome. During this time, I couldn't sleep, sit or focus at work. Mr. Intelligent supported me by going to many different doctors and providing me comfort, empathy and understanding. I fell in love with him at this point and that's when we started to discuss marriage. We weren't ready for marriage but we both truly believed we loved each other. As we got closer and deeper into our relationship and discussing our lives together, we hit a nerve in regards to religion; we weren't on the same page about walking with God or our beliefs. Once we both realized that we were not on the same page when it came to our Christian or Non-Christian beliefs, we decided to pump the breaks on our decision to marry. It hurt my heart but I knew God had my back and it would make sense one day…As we decided we would take one day at a time and maybe things would change but the problem was that he was chosen to go represent the Air Force at the Presidential Inauguration in D.C and I was headed to my next base in Florida. So we decided to go our separate ways and I just didn't know how I would go on. I took him to the airport so he can go to Washington D.C. and as I was driving back to my dorm room my heart was torn; I was devasted that we were done. No more dancing, singing and loving on each other. No more Burger King runs or silly dance offs we would have. I didn't know how to be ok but I knew I would be ok! As I departed Germany; I was excited to move to Florida I always wanted to live in Florida little did I know I was really moving to Lower Alabama! The Base was close to a Papermill Factory; what that meant was that it smelled like dog poop all the time! The city was quite boring; besides the two good clubs that I enjoyed because they played good hip hop; there wasn't anything I liked in that city. Needless to say, as soon as I moved there I can tell: I was not going to like it! This was the first time I was actually in a maintenance squadron; I usually worked in a personnel office or medical building. This time I was with the airplane fighters and maintainers that kept our airplanes up to par. This was definitely different than any other place I was at before. I was quickly thrown in charge of two airman that were actually higher ranking then me but I had a line number for Staff Sergeant; this was extremely challenging and uncomfortable. So, I'm at this new base: Not liking my job, not liking my new town I call home and heartbroken. When is the best time for the devil to throw a rebound into a desperate 24-year-old females life? After she is heartbroken and alone in a new city and job! Ladies!!! This is when you must be aware; right after a deep heart break you must be vigilant! This is when the devil will sneak in and distract you from your hurt feelings and persuade you with this new guy that is sooo amazing, kind, attentive, funny and thoughtful. You see;

but what happens when we are heart broken and our vision is blurry is that we forget our original hearts desires because were so focused on not being alone; that we will not make authentic decisions. This is when we get into a "rebound" situation. The technical explanation of a "rebound guy or relationship" is this: some person you use to get over the person you just broke up with. They'll never be enough but they can be an okay distraction. (Urban Dictionary, 1999)

Usually a relationship that happens after our heart is ripped out of our chest is short-lived; simply because we are grabbing on to anything that will take our minds off of our broken hearts! This was my exact situation with Mr. Rican. He was nice, attentive, from the east coast, fun and easy to get along with but he was not in any way shape or form my type but I was hurt, alone and heartbroken from my last relationship and I missed the Man I was going to marry terribly so I jumped into the arms of another human being that was breathing. Ladies! HUGE MISTAKE! There's a saying that goes like this: In order to get over one man you need to get under another man! Sorry! That's so wrong it should go like this: In order to heal from your pain and become a whole woman you should consciously separate yourself from others and seek solitude with one's thoughts, feelings and desires; in order to be the best version of oneself! As me and Mr. Rican talked more and more at work we decided to date and soon after we were dating; we decided to get married! I look back and I remember the weekend of our wedding like it was yesterday; I was on base getting ready to make a right-hand turn and as I stood looking at the stop sign, I thought... I do not want to get married and then quickly thought you have all these people in town that have spent their money and time and you cannot disrespect them by sending them home!! All I kept thinking was there's no way I can call this wedding off and not look like I have all my ducks in a row! On paper Mr. Rican is a good guy so I'll be alright! He's established, respectful, accomplished, financially stable and has an excellent personality. If I were to call it off now; I could be making a HUGE mistake because he's willing to love me and make a commitment to marry me. Even though I felt deep down inside that he was a rebound, I was not in love with him and truly I was still in love with Mr. Intelligent! I knew that Mr. Intelligent and I were not going to be an item; I felt he left me because he didn't want to serve my God and move forward and marry me. I felt dismissed by him because of my beliefs. I felt safe on my decision to marry Mr. Rican; he was safe and I knew for sure that he loved me more than I loved him. As long as he loved me more than I loved him I will not get hurt! So as I gathered all my thoughts sitting at this stop sign I still chose to move forward and make my right hand turn and marry Mr. Rican. As I was in turmoil in my mind that very day Mr. Intelligent sent me an email to my work account and asked to talk to me about some decisions, he was contemplating on making in regards to moving forward with a girlfriend he had. Little did he know I was preparing for my wedding weekend with doubts and yearning for Mr. Intelligent deep in my heart. Now that I look back God was directing my steps even though I was going the wrong way; he still protected me through my mistakes. It was evident that I would not stay married to Mr. Rican since I was not emotionally complete or healed before I married him. Our marriage lasted one year and I chose to get divorced and move out. Mr. Rican was an amazing husband and friend but I was the one that needed healing before I involved another human being in my dysfunctional love life. The real problem was that I was a runner instead of confronting my deep issues of heartbreak, loneliness, abandonment, insecurities and the dysfunction from my childhood; I would just get into another relationship! Year after year, month after month and day after day; I ran! After this divorce It didn't stop my running away. My behavior was actually not any different; there was still lessons God would choose to teach me through more heartbreaks and one more marriage!

Knowledge Nugget:

God purposely left me to endure pain after pain FACE to FACE so I could properly HEAL!

Four

CELIBACY

> "Flee from sexual immorality. Every other sin a person commits is outside the body, but the sexually immoral person sins against his own body. Or do you not know that your body is a temple of the Holy Spirit within you, whom you have from God? You are not your own, for you were bought with a price. So glorify God in your body." 1 Cor 6:18-20 New International Version (NIV)

THE MOMENT I SAW MR. Brown Sugar he immediately got my attention because he had an east coast swag, perfect teeth, Atlantic Ocean waves on his head, a fade that was on point, smelled like fresh cocoa butter and had a perfect complexion of brown sugar. I was mesmerized but I kept my liking of him to myself; I admired him from afar. We were both on the Honor Guard Team for the Air Force and sometimes we went on funeral details together so we would talk about life and the type of music we liked. A couple of times we had to share food or clothes because it was either raining, sleeting or beyond hot outside! I felt as if he had a liking to me as well but he was more reserved so I stood in the friend zone. I knew I was in the friend zone the day he called me and asked me for advice for this girl he was dating. I was upset inside my heart but I knew that he had no clue I was interested in him so I gave him friendly advice and prayed they didn't last. After a couple of months of details and talking to each other we went out to lunch then lunch turned into dinner then dinner turned into couples events then we ended up dating. LADIES! Yet again no conversations about our moral compasses or our standards; we just jumped into a relationship. Now Mr. Brown Sugar was younger than me about 8 years younger; this may not be too many years but for our ages it was. He was in his early 20's. He was stepping into his manhood and I was ready to settle down again; because by now I'm way passed my checklist of lifetime milestones. I AGAIN ignored all of the red flags of no deep conversations and our age difference. I felt loved and admired and I wanted to continue to receive those feelings. In all honesty I was too selfish to put my insecurities aside by having my ego stroked; I just allowed the events of his admiration rule my life; yet again! We dated for about six months and during those 6 months I attended a Women's Conference called "Chosen" and this conference changed my view on Celibacy for the rest of my life. I have always had a struggle with practicing celibacy on purpose but at this conference the Holy Spirit placed on my heart that I will not grow spiritually if I continue to have sex without being fully committed by marriage. The importance of Celibacy goes deeper than what the world presents if at any time it does discuss Celibacy. The definition of **Celibacy** that I'm referring to here is: to abstain from engaging in any sexual activity, usually for religious reasons; another behavior that can be practiced is: **Abstinence** which refers to the strict avoidance of all forms of sexual activity for any reason. ("Celibacy", n.d.)

The Biblical Interpretation: 1 Corinthians 7:1-3; Common English Bible (CEB) "It's good for a man not to have sex with a woman." Each man should have his own wife, and each woman should have her own husband because of sexual immorality. The definition of sexual immorality is the engagement in sexual acts outside of the commitment of marriage which is for the purpose of creating life. (Christian Editorial Staff; 2016) God strategically made women for men and their purpose was to reproduce human life and multiply; not to have sexual acts just to have "fun". Having "fun" that involves sex can lead to the transference of spirits of bondage, addiction, jealousy, anger, depression or any unhealthy characteristic your sexual partner is carrying as their burdens or their bondages. When we choose to engage in sexual activity with another human being that has a past of anxiety, insecurities, envy or pride it will definitely flow into our spirit. Another negative aspect of sexual intercourse without the boundaries of marriage is that the act of sex or the person or persons that is engaging in your sexual act can become your Idol! God is a jealous God; he does not want no other place or thing to be your Idol... but him! God has an order in place for a specific reason; he wants us to know our purpose and to be living for the will God; the will that he has for us. If we are distracted by earthly Idols then we cannot grow spiritually with God or enhance our skills for the kingdom of God. It's also very important to practice celibacy because you want to discover the character of the man your dating. You want to see him throughout his day and his relationship with God. It's important that the two of you pray together, read the word together, help the community together and bring the lost to the throne of God TOGETHER. The bible says in 2 Corinthians 6:14 New International Version (NIV) "Do not be yoked together with unbelievers. For what do righteousness and wickedness have in common? Or what fellowship can light have with darkness?" In simple terms; while you are a saved woman of God and you are dating; how can a woman that is a woman of God, prayer is her secret weapon, her Bible is the answer to her life problems and she is consistently on her knees praying to her father in heaven and her savior Jesus Christ; then.... choose to be with a man that doesn't want to seek God or pray to the God she does! That is a disaster of resentment, bitterness, conflict and confusion waiting to erupt. When two saved people serve the same God, they both can go to God with their problems, confusions, trials and anger. God will use the Holy Spirit to guide them along the right path.

    Another reason why celibacy is important is because we can no longer show our affection by the act of sex but we are forced to physically do actions of love and sit down and spend quality time with each other. Without sex you can completely focus by communicating in a deep level of love for one another. The act of sex is a gift given to us after marriage; it's icing on the cake after two souls are united under God.

    My spirit always felt guilt when I would take action in the act of sex before marriage and after leaving this conference my spirit was awaken to no longer have sex with Mr. Brown Sugar unless we were married! As I went to his house after a long weekend of the teachings of celibacy and sexual immorality; I was fearful but ready to make my stance in the ground to be committed to God by practicing celibacy. I knew I would be taking a risk by asking this 20 something year old young man that I just started having relations with... to now... not engage in any sexual activity until we are married. Mr. Brown Sugar was an active young man sexually; and he had plenty of options and not to mention he was not an active man of God so how could I ask him to believe in morals that he didn't even have any knowledge of. I knew I was asking him to make a big commitment to a God and a Bible that he never engaged in but I had to stand up for what God laid in my spirit. As I told him my new vow to remain celibate; time stood still as he looked at me and I saw a range of emotions showed up in his face. He paused as he told me he needed time to think about this new way of living in our relationship. I did just that I gave him time as I was weeping in my car driving home, I knew it was the right thing to do. A couple of days passed and he called me to tell me he doesn't know how he will be celibate but he loves me and he will give me his best. I was ecstatic but scared at the same time. A couple of months passed and him and I were not agreeing on anything so we decided to take time apart; during this time, he ended up getting orders to Germany. I was shocked but I knew if we were meant to be together then him being overseas will test our love and determine if we were meant to be back together. As he went off to Germany, I was hurt but I knew it was time for me to focus on my healing and to let go of my past.

During the time Mr. Brown Sugar was gone a friend of mine played match maker and linked me up with a friend of his by giving him my number. Mr. Smoothtalker is his name. He was smooth with words, his clothes, his tactics and his flirtatious attributes. What's funny is that Mr. Smoothtalker was in my squadron but I was never attracted to him because I was in a relationship with Mr. Brown Sugar but a lot of girls were attracted to him and they would point him out to me every time we saw him in the gym. One day a friend of mine sent me an email hooking me up with his "older" friend but I had no idea it was Mr. Smoothtalker; then I received an email from him. It only took a couple of emails between the two of us before Mr. Smoothtalker asked to take me out. Our first date was at Joes Crabshack and it was interesting to be on a date with a man that's a decade older than me. Now trust me he didn't look his age but the problem is that I have always looked like a teenager all my life. I'm excited that it will pay off once I'm 60 years old and I will look 40 but, in this situation, I felt like I was a kid dating an old man. I knew he didn't mind but it lingered in the back of my head. Ladies!! Listen to me… this was my own personal insecurities stepping in whispering in my ear "Your not good enough for this accomplished, good looking, intelligent older man"! This was my problem; I was jumping into being in love with another human being instead of being inlove with myself! I was escaping the loneliness and hurt from Mr. Brown Sugar moving to Germany. So at the end of the night of my first date with Mr. Smoothtalker and as he approached to drop me off he says "I hope you know I'm a grown man that likes to do grown things" I said "that's good and I'm grown too" as I closed the door to his truck and walked into my house by myself. I was thinking who he thinks he is?! Now in this moment LADIES!! I should've stopped and reflected on the Chosen Conference I attended 2 years earlier; I should've reminded myself by writing Post it's all around me that I was practicing Celibacy! I needed to be reminded of the word in regards to sexual immorality and the revelation the Holy Spirit brought on me during that conference. The commitment I made to God should've instantly came to my mind when he stated that "He was Grown and liked to do Grown Things"; instead my brain went back to its regular programming which was all the statements my nana ingrained into my brain while I was growing up. She raised me with high standards in regards to dating men that had a good career, money and looked good. She always lectured me to keep a lock on my girl aka my kitty kat unless a man earned it. She taught me the carnal way of not giving up my "goodies". This was her statement on dating and having intercourse "Look… it takes money and time to keep your girl clean and if he ain't giving you no money or time then he can't get none". As I got older my three rules in dating and sexual activity were: 1. We must be in a relationship 2. We have to be together for 60-90 days or more 3. Does my potential boyfriend spend time or money on me? If any of these requirements were not met then it was time to break up and keep it moving. (needless to say I wish I knew what the Bible said about intercourse). I wish I learned the real meaning of love before I allowed my heart to get used, abused and thrown to the floor. I was a 28 yr. old little girl roaming the streets of love that included wolves and devils clothed in sheep clothing. Me and Mr. Smoothtalker went on a couple more dates to add up to 3 months and I "assumed" big mistake that women make, we "assume" that the guy is ready to be in a relationship with us if he's still going out to dinners and participating in couple-like activities. The reality was he was a grown man taking anything he could from me with no commitments or titles and guess what… I allowed him to!!! Not only did I allow it… I willingly gave it to him and disregarded my rules, desires or morals on celibacy. BIG MISTAKE! Ladies!! We tend to do this HUGE MISTAKE… we ignore our morals just to feel admired or loved. This act of injustice we do to ourselves creates a level of disrespect, humiliation and opens a door for the enemy to come in and wreak havoc on our path that God has pre-destined us for; BEFORE WE WERE ON THIS EARTH!

As the months went by; Mr. Smoothtalker and I were hanging out more; meaning having relations as if we were in a committed relationship but we absolutely were not! In my mind, yet again ladies please hear me when I say "In my mind" because that's what the majority of women that are in a "Friends With Benefits" situation do but they do not want to admit it. They assume or act like they are in an actual committed relationship! My mind was insinuating that but I was too scared to ask him so I still "played along" meaning going on dates, sleeping with him, cooking for him, dressing up for him, going on trips with him, renting hotel rooms on weekend get-a-ways with him but I never asked him "Why is your phone always face down?" or "Are we in a committed relationship?" My fear was that I would irritate him enough to not spend some nights with me or not call me. This went on for months, Yes!! Months of a non but serious relationship…. mind you I was the only one that believed we were serious. He then got sent away on a deployment and the emails were far and few in between but I didn't catch the hint. I kept mailing him packages and desperately awaiting a response and of course he would reply with an email thanking me but no statements about a commitment or that he loved me. I knew I was in love with him actually I told him right before he left in his kitchen. As I was sobbing and desperately trying to get a commitment from him; he decided to question my intentions. He stated "how do I know that you aren't with me because of my rank" I stopped and had to gather my thoughts and said to myself... it's not like you're the president or I'm reaping the benefits of his rank... he wasn't paying my bills!!! But little did I not realize that this statement was going to be the first of many derailing tactics that he would play for the next 7 years; on and off! I entertained the non-sense and whatever type of activity or "date" he would take me on. The sad thing was that some of the dates were not even dates; that meant he was cooking one of my favorite meals and staying in for the night. This is not a REAL DATE; but I was too blind to see clearly. My problem was that I was inlove with him. I kept practicing over and over again that once he returned from his deployment I would draw the line and he would have to make a decision on making a commitment to me. Needless to say, when he returned from his deployment; he didn't even reach out to me till I saw his car parked at the bank! Yes, LADIES HUGE SIGN! Another man I entertained that did not make a commitment to me or even contact me after he was gone for 6 months. This opened my eyes and I decided to let go and move on. I chose to leave him alone in any way possible. I couldn't allow him to hurt me like that again so I chose to not call or see him. I truly was hurt but I learned in this situation to NEVER believe WORDS, it's the actions of love that prove their commitment to you and Mr. Smooth Talker was not sacrificing or displaying any actions in regards to love at all! It's sad that I allowed the delusional little girl to convince me to settle with the non-emotional man that was in my life. In the end, Mr. Smoothtalker and I were Friends with Benefits and I talked myself into believing that he was my boyfriend! As I reflected back and thought to myself: If I would've stood on my foundation that was firm in Jesus Christ and his word; none of the heartache I allowed to happen with Mr. Smoothtalker or the insecurities I developed while dating him; would've happened!! BUT GOD! All of the insecurities that were pulled out by Mr. Smoothtalker's non-present attitude; arose an awakening inside me that I would need in years to come!

Knowledge Nugget:

I should've let God's word rule me instead of my heart run me!!

Five

DATE YOURSELF

Scripture: "Love is patient, love is kind. It does not envy, it does not boast, it is not proud. ⁵It does not dishonor others, it is not self-seeking, it is not easily angered, it keeps no record of wrongs. ⁶Love does not delight in evil but rejoices with the truth. ⁷It always protects, always trusts, always hopes, always perseveres." 1 Corinthians 13:4-8; New International Version (NIV)

THE MOMENT I SAW MR. ROMANTIC it was like time stood still. You see I always had a quick liking for a man that had a caramel complexion, authoritarian personality and successfully accomplished. As soon as Mr. Romantic walked into my office; I said to myself: he seems like a motivated young Senior Non-Commissioned Officer (SNCO) I would like to get to know. A couple of months passed by and he ended up being a guest speaker at a leadership course I was taking. The moment he opened his mouth to speak and only 5 minutes into the briefing I was so impressed with his "Go get em" mentality and his intelligence. I immediately sent a text to one of my friends and told her that this young accomplished SNCO was moving to her base and he would be a good mentor for her. As time went on him and I became associates because he needed help with his move. Now looking back, we were both two souls wanting to be understood because we weren't in our past. I started telling him my future goals of exiting the military and pursuing my radio and broadcasting career. He tried to persuade me to re-enlist in the military but once I explained my future goals; he supported my decision. We both fasted together and prayed that my early separation package would get approved. Soon after; it did! I remember us connecting spiritually and talking about our spiritual journey from our childhood to our current day. We would talk and talk for hours on end about everything. I loved the fact that Mr. Romantic always had empathy for my health, career choices and family; he was always an excellent listener. I remember the day he gave up on me internally about my interest in him. One day we went to lunch and we were talking about pretty celebrities and I told him Kim Kardashian was a beautiful woman along with Jennifer Lopez. He stated that he didn't think Kim was but Jlo was pretty and he asked me what male celebrities do I like: I said Tall, 6 foot, determined, beautiful smile and built like L.L. Cool J. He said in that moment he knew we would only be friends. If he only knew I was so nervous to sit there and talk to him on a Personal level. He was a young, decorated and accomplished SNCO that had high goals and I admired his determination. I actually was intimidated because I was a little staff sergeant with dreams of exiting the military and to move back home; while he was preparing for the next highest rank with only 13 years in the Military! The man he was I found so attractive even though he wasn't 6 foot but he was understanding, supportive, communicated openly, giving, kind, humble, excellent father, generous with gifts and we liked the same music. He would help me study for my tests and exams while I was in college. He would buy special food for me so whenever I came over, I had my snacks. As time went on, we were just two friends getting to know each other. Until one day we came back from a lounge and we were talking in the garage and he leaned over and kissed me. I was in shock! He caught me off guard! I didn't know what to say?? I did know what I felt!! I felt a rush of emotions and thoughts. I just knew that he was different. He listened and he cared for me in a different manner than any other man. He then looked at me and said: you better hurry your friend is waiting for you in the car. So I go… okay bye. The next day we talked a little bit but not much. I didn't know what to say or how to feel. I wasn't fully ready for more emotions and another relationship. But the way I love and the hopeless romantic I am; I definitely wasn't going to give up on love. So, I said to myself; I'm scared, worried but I'm going all in! Ladies!!!! That's the problem right there. I wasn't thinking rationally. I was allowing my feelings and heart... rule my actions and life. I needed to stay his friend and get to know him longer to see if he or I wanted any relationship! We just got out of marriages and did not enjoy our singleness long enough. We didn't allow that to stop ourselves from falling in love and once we were in love it was all over. Mr. Romantic was just that "Romantic" in every way possible. He would dedicate songs to me as we danced in the living room and enjoyed a candle lit dinner. He would plan date nights with roses and one on one time where we would have deep conversations. On my birthday week every year he would plan a week filled with presents, trips and surprises throughout the whole week. One year while I was visiting him in Japan for my birthday he took me to 3 trips; all surprises. I loved that about him!!! He was that dude that investigated my inner desires and made sure to make them happen. We walked up Mount Fiji, we went on a boat ride around one of the islands by Japan and we went to this amazing Navy hotel and restaurant which by the way we were the only ones in that restaurant. It was breath taking; looking back at that day now and it's so depressing to say that I thought since we were the only people in the restaurant that Mr. Romantic was going to PROPOSE! The joke was on me! You know LADIES... we always make up a story in our heads about the man we are with. The RED SIGNS are there but we just don't choose to see them! You see once Mr. Romantic got orders to Japan and I got accepted to Radio and Tv Broadcasting School I should've known that long distance relationships DO NOT WORK; but I was naïve and believed in our love. As he went off overseas and I moved back to New Jersey the communication between us dwindled but I still was planning to go see him and buying outfits to look amazing. I was so excited to go see my non communicating boyfriend. Since he still wanted me to go and spend the month with him, I believed that he still wanted to be in a relationship with me. My trip to go see him went amazing but soon after I returned back home our relationship went back to how it was before I visited him. Fewer messages, phone calls and emails; I could sense that there was distance between us and I did not want to admit that!! He was yet again being distant but I had to be honest with myself. After one night of me calling Mr. Romantic continuously and not being able to get a hold of him I knew we were over. When he finally called me back and told me that we needed space because I was getting to be too much. I felt like the world ended... I was devasted; my heart stopped. As we both went our separate ways we never stopped talking and whenever he was in the states, I would fly to whichever state he was at and allow my heart to get excited and believe that if I was good enough, he would want us to get back together. LADIES!!! Read again what I just said "If I was GOOD ENOUGH"; the fact is... my reality of who I was in his life and what I meant to him was SKEWED. What I mean by that is he didn't love me to the magnitude that I deeply loved him and it didn't matter how "good" I was in his presence. His mind was made up about our status and I wasn't the woman he was EVER going to commit to again or marry!! That was the reality but I continuously believed that since he made time for me and showered me with little gifts here and there that he did want me in his future!! That wasn't the case; he just didn't mine "kicking it with me" time after time. LADIES!!! I beg you to please don't ignore the man in your life and his true motives and actions. Be honest; ask questions in regards to your future!! Don't play yourself; just for a good date or weekend trip! What I should've been doing is: DATING MYSELF! Enjoying my alone time and discovering the woman I was destined to be! The importance for a woman to know her worth and her value as a human being on this earth outweighs any man's love! God pre-ordained each woman with a specific destiny and purpose to accomplish on this earth. It's our job to take the time alone in order for God to speak to us and to pour into us the love, guidance and virtue we were meant to embrace and grow from. Instead I was riding the coattails of my ex-boyfriend desperately wanting him to ask me to be his girlfriend... AGAIN! Well that didn't happen instead month after month I chose to go wherever he was sent by the military. This went on for two more years and one of the last trips I went to meet him in Baltimore after 6 months of him being deployed to Afghanistan and I was so excited to see him and embrace my best friend. My butterflies were still just as active as they were the first date we went on but too bad the butterflies only lasted for Mr. Romantic for about a year. His career was his top priority and in no way shape or form did he allow me to ask him questions "outside the boundaries of our relationship" that was the exact response he sent me in a 3 page email 5 days after he decided to part ways with me for the second time on Oct 31st 2013. The day before; Oct 30th, 2013 as I got my outfit ready and flew to D.C. airport and nervously awaited the arrival of my Mr. Romantic; the love I believed was my ONE and only love. I was excited to see him and I imagined he would be just as excited to see me. You see I love hard and since he did at the beginning of our relationship I believed; regardless of the red flags; that "Mr. Romantic" loved me just as much as our first year. He then arrived with all the soldiers at the same time and I'm standing there with Wives, Mothers, children and girlfriends... then there's ME with my big heart on my chest and no TITLE no STATUS; just a friend waiting for a friend. As he walked out, I could hear my heart beating a million miles a minute and sweat slowly forming on my hands. He gives me a weak hug and seemed not at least a bit amused with me. He was quiet the majority of the walk to the car then to the restaurant and we get to the hotel and silence was my best friend. You see now that I have my Master's degree in counseling; I understand that his silence had nothing to do with me; actually, nothing at all! He was just a military member that was deployed in a war zone and he had to decompress his feelings and emotions; never the less I was ignorant, selfish and overly sensitive. The reality is: if he didn't want me to be in his presence he would've never told me when he was landing and never would've allowed me to come... PERIOD! It's so sad how co-dependent I was on him to make ME FEEL whole, worthy and wanted. I know now NO ONE can make me feel anything; we as women must take the time to invest the love into our own soul and all of the appropriate amount of worth and value will be deposited into us; from God!

The next morning, I tried to interact as much as possible but he was distant as we went to visit his grandmother and father; his convos with me were limited. I felt rejected and alone in my excitement to see him. As the night went on, he springs on me my 3-day trip was a 2 days trip because he was going to see his "friend" (which is an EX) and I flipped. Now, I am a reserved female for a long time until I can't hold back anymore of my feelings or emotions. While I'm yelling in the car looking probably like a maniac, he's just sitting there quiet then leaves me in the car as I'm sobbing and he walked up to the room. The problem is that I OVER EXAGGERATED MY ROLE in his life and sometimes... well, most of the time women assume their role and presence in a man's life without confronting him and asking for clarification. We tend to believe if he allows us in his life and spends time with us that we are their "woman" but that's not the case. Men think on a different wave length then us, their brains are simple. Majority of the time men just spend time with women when they don't want to be alone at the moment so they will choose from their list of likings of women and hang out with them more often than not and this is when the woman begins to think and plan their whole life together when the man just wants to go to the movies or Netflix and chill. My problem was that I believed in our "love" I thought it was still alive. I didn't look at the non-verbals of him not planning for us to spend time or book trips together. I was living in a fantasy; made up world of what we used to be. Then that day; all my made-up illusions of us came crashing down and I was face to face with the ugly truth. I was in-love with Mr. Romantic and willing to cross oceans and he just enjoyed my company whenever we could make time to be around each other. His specific words were "Were not in a relationship and you don't need to ask me questions in regards to my personal life". He then stated that I would catch the next flight out. As it would be my luck there was a Nor Easter so I couldn't fly out of any airports till the following day. He was stuck with me and I was stuck with him unfortunately. We tried our best and didn't kill each other and no other arguments happened. As I left the next day I sobbed as I hugged him goodbye and knew this was it. You better pull yourself together he is not sobbing because your leaving he's actually excited about his next trip to see his ex-girlfriend as your depressed self is getting on that plane and I had no idea what was ahead of me. This situation would be another heartbreak to go into my journal; one of many; in my 33 years of life. On that long plane ride home which in my mind took days and in actual distance time it took 1 hour in a half. I thought about all that I have given to Mr. Romantic and what I didn't do in my previous marriage, I thought how I truly loved him and it seemed as if my love was and is never allowed to grow into its fruition. I thought about all the traveling I did for this man and wondered why did I accept so little in exchange for my A LOT. I started to think about how we began and why I allowed myself to fall so hard. I allowed the little I received from Mr. Romantic and in no means, it was his fault; his behavior continued on what I ALLOWED. This heartbreak was MY FAULT! I allowed the non-committed relationship to last because I was not secure in who I was, what I wanted and what I deserved. I didn't take the time to DATE MYSELF!

You see being in love floods our brains with chemicals that induce feelings of everything from pleasure to intense focus and attachment. Now once you are in love; blood begins to flow to the pleasure center of the brain. This feeling causes an over obsessive compulsive behavior towards the man that your involved with. Since all the emotions are happiness, we do not want these emotions to end and in our brain it's a happy place but then when the negative chemicals are responding to the behavior of the man that you believed would be your forever our body goes into a fight or flight response. Internally our heart is palpitating supper fast and our minds is trying to cope with the stress of a heartbreak and making a plan to flee this emotion. That was the stage in my life I was at in that plane ride home; I asked myself: am I going to respond in a Fight or Flight reaction. I came to the reality that Mr. Romantic loved me to the best of his ability. I chose to consciously accept his love or lack of attention and by any means I allowed the disconnect to continue for longer than it should have! I give thanks to God for giving me an amazing romantic guy for the 2.5 years we truly enjoyed each other. Now the long road to recovery from a heartbreak took: Time. Energy. Discipline. Evaluation and Self Love! I lost my best friend, my main squeeze, my inspiration, my joke buddy, my travel partner and the man I believed I would be with forever. He took care of me selflessly when I was sick after my bladder surgery, he loved me in all of my mess, he encouraged me to go for my dreams of radio and to never give up on myself and he always had my back financially. I didn't know how I would be ok with that void in my life but deep in my heart I felt he obviously is totally ok with losing all that I was to him and for that I respected my soul and chose to heal and move on. My heart deserved healing and my body deserved peace. I started to do some things on my own and enjoyed them; I worked hard and endless hours at Sirius XM radio in the city and was going to college to receive my Bachelors in Christian Ministry. All my hard work payed off and I received an ON-AIR WEEKEND GIG in South Jersey on "Ocean Counties Only hit Music Station" I was so grateful and excited to finally start my radio career.

Mr. Romantic reached out to me on holidays but that was it. The first conversation we had since the departure the year prior in Baltimore; was the first weekend I was going to be on air. He called to congratulate me and I was so grateful for his phone call and I got to speak to his kids which I loved and missed and I knew that in some way shape or form that we had an understanding and we would always have a connection but I knew I had to let go and I chose to do that. The complete process took a total of 5 lonnnnnngggg years! Till this day we have a low-level friendship and for that I'm grateful but the love we shared was memorable and I **NAMASTE** to that!

During my healing season and new move to Jersey I met this amazing amazing sweet, handsome soul. A soul that I never never encountered before in my life!

It was Valentine's Day the day I received a phonecall from Mr. Perfect. I'll never forget that day because two strangers that never spoke or met each other ended up having a two-hour conversation about life. You see my aunt knew Mr. Perfect for years and he always would look at her myspace page while they were on break at their job and since the first day he saw my picture on her page he stated "that's my wife". My aunt always ignored his comments until 3 years into him asking her for my number she finally gave in. He said he wanted to talk to me because he knew that there was something, I had that he wanted. So, my aunt asked me if she could give him my number; I thought about it and said well he would be a friend so yes you can give him my number. Once we hung up from our first conversation, he told me later that he felt a peace afterwards like a breath of fresh air. I felt as if a man was hearing me with the intent to listen and cast no judgement but to be that confidant to me. I also felt that this man experienced a lot in his life and chooses to learn from each obstacle and becomes better from his past. I felt as if he was an old soul; just like me! I also enjoyed the fact that Mr. Perfect was a man that was from the same state and inner city as me so we connected on a deeper level than any other man. Now he wasn't prior military so I found it interesting that we vibed so well and easily. I believe with my heart that we connected because he was vulnerable with me and I was with him. Mind you I never meet this man but we began to talk everyday until our first encounter which was a month later. The moment I saw Mr. Perfect, that's what I saw... perfection in reality. The curve of his lips in his smile, the cleanliness of his teeth, his adorable laughter, his height that matched the width of his back, he was 6ft one and wore Timberland boots but the kicker was that he had an east coast swag to him that I loved. Now if you re-read what caught my attention about Mr. Perfect the day I met him and tell me if you see God in any one of those attributes or that he was a devoted member of following Jesus Christ or I loved the way he prayed before our meals. NO! LADIES!!! LISTEN and read this carefully!! That is exactly how the enemy lures us into satisfying our fleshly desires. Now don't get me wrong Mr. Perfect is humble, kind, amazing father, son and human being but he was still young and trying to identify what his purpose was in God or Allah. He only knew and practiced the Muslim religion. He wasn't a devout Muslim neither because him and I would talk about God and he would ask for me to pray for him to my savior. He knew the word and would send me prayers to encourage me at times as well. If you know a devout muslin (like my Dad) they will engage in a conversation involving another religion but would never steer away from Allah. He would send me prayers involving my God and not Allah. I could always lean on him for advice or wise words on life. He never talked down to me or ridiculed my mistakes or actions. I felt peace whenever I talked to him or was in his presence. He was my anchor; he is the man I would go to if I needed words of encouragement or motivation, he was the person I would call FIRST. Our friendship consisted of numerous hours on the phone or in person hanging out at one of my favorite restaurants. YOU SEE… during this time I should've been focusing on new places and hobbies to pick up on my own. I should've been exploring New York City on my own; not spending time with another man and allowing my feelings to get connected with another soul! Instead I chose to emotionally get involved; yet again with another man that was emotionally unavailable! LADIES!! This is what we do we get so entangled in the motions of him "acting" like he wants a true commitment when he is taking one day at a time; enjoying a non-committed and non-sexual friendship!

After more time we spent together; I realized that I could be thinking about a certain feeling or an attitude about a situation and all he needed to do was to look at my face and he knew my feelings, thoughts and assumptions. Before I could explain my feelings on a certain situation he would interject and know exactly what route I was going to embark upon. I enjoyed our time together and year after year of long conversations; I feel in love. I feel in love with a man that was perfect to me; he was understanding, transparent, vulnerable, respectful, thoughtful friend, consistent father, selfless son, humble, super cute, sexy swag but he was in a relationship so for 4 years I did not express my feelings. I truly enjoyed our friendship until our friendship turned into an emotional relationship. One day he asked to go with me to my friends retirement ceremony in Texas. I knew that would be challenging but I knew my level of discipline along with his level of respect for me; we would be good. As we traveled to Texas and enjoyed the area and the retirement; two souls respected each other's boundaries and I was proud. We stood talking early into the morning and ended it with an unexpected kiss!! I then knew nope we gotta go and that's what we did; got up and ready and headed to the airport. I remember while we were headed back we had a good flight but my feelings were running wild and I knew I had to contain them or they would engulf my whole being. I pulled back for a while and he noticed I developed strong feelings for him and just like we always did we talked about it and decided to not spend time together so we didn't, we always talked on the phone but for a couple of months we didn't see each other. I knew in my heart that it was best for me to step away from him; I knew that he needed time to be single and to decide if I was the next relationship he wanted. As time went on; we started seeing each other again and one night after us having a deep conversation on our situation, our possible future and our feelings; I lost it. I screamed at him and said NO MORE... I LOVE YOU AND YOU DON'T WANT TO MAKE MOVES! I slammed his car door and went into my house. I was so mad that I allowed my true feelings to show! I was always good at keeping my emotions together and definitely not allowing him to know my heart. I was disappointed in myself! At this point; I knew I'm not going to be suckered into another conversation, long dinners and intimate nightcaps. I stood away from Mr. Perfect and did not answer his phonecalls for 6 months! I decided I was moving back to Texas to pursue my Masters in Counseling and I was leaving my feelings and Mr. Perfect in New Jersey. As I was preparing for my move, I ended up in the hospital due to anxiety and a heart condition that I didn't know about. My stay in the hospital was a week long and one day as I was watching TV; Mr. Perfect surprised me in my hospital room. My heart machine starting beeping super-fast and the nurse ran inside to check my heart machine; it was the most embarrassing moment in my life.

I was laying in a bed for 4 days, no bath, in a hospital gown, no make up and my heart literally beating a million beats a minute as Mr. Perfect is standing there worried but enjoying the fact that HE made my heart beat so fast! I had to take time to take deep breaths in order for my heart to calm down and Mr. Perfect had to leave the room for a while. As he came back he expressed to me how my aunt called him and told him I was in the hospital and he wanted to see me. I told him he didn't have to but he insisted that he cared about me and no matter what; he will never leave me alone. I listened and left that conversation right there; in no way shape or form was I in the right state of mind to discuss my "feelings". After I was released from the hospital I moved to Texas. After two years of deep conversations that involved tears and tough decisions Mr. Perfect had to make; he finally tells me "I LOVE U 4 EVER AND ANOTHER YEAR OF LIFE" but "I cannot be the man that you need me to be. I don't want to lose you as my friend because I wouldn't meet up to your expectations as your boyfriend. He starts to explain that he doesn't feel that I would need him because I am not "broken" he states your strong and independent and I'm not there yet. He states; I think your too good of a friend or woman to me; to lose. I know I would mess it up with us and I have to be honest with you!" In that moment I felt two strong emotions RESPECT and DISAPPOINTMENT! I respect him for speaking his truth but disappointment because we fit together like a glove in all ways and we would NEVER be together. After months of praying and reflecting, God showed me that I needed a man to know what he wanted and a man that wanted to take over the world with me. A man that wouldn't take the chance on losing me forever! He was Mr. Perfect but just not my Mr. Perfect Guy and that was ok!

<u>Knowledge Nugget:</u>

<u>Love lost is not really a LOVE LOST it's a removal of what love should not be in your life! You don't lose a LOVE that is meant for you! If the love of your life walks away then He was just a counterfeit for what God has prepared for you!</u>

Six

SUBMISSION

Scripture: "Submit yourselves therefore to God. Resist the devil, and he will flee from you." James 4:7-10 New International Version (NIV)

SUBMISSION: THIS WORD ALONE I never knew what it truly meant until a season of loss in my life and servanthood. I had to be SUB to the MISSION of the ultimate plans of Christ VS. the plans that I had envisioned for my own life. The moment I had to put my plans down and SURRENDER to the purpose and destiny God sacrificed his son for us.

I grew up in a home where there was no submission to no one. God, Christ or the Church was not the head of our home. There was no Husband, Uncle or Father present to show my brother, sister or me the acts of submission. So, I was living in a home where I didn't know the acts of submission in regards to a male and definitely didn't know the role of becoming SUB to the Mission of Christ. As I got older the military taught me a portion of submission to commanders, supervisors and the mission of the Air Force; which was to protect this nation. I became accustomed to submitting to authority; even when I was a child. I didn't like anyone calling my attention to anything I have done wrong and definitely didn't like getting in trouble as a child. But when it came to authority in regards to my personal desires or a man in my home; now that was a different level of submission to me. I viewed submissive women as WEAK women; that is so not the case if submission is in a healthy manner. The Bible states in Titus 3:1 "To respect the government and be law-abiding, always be ready to lend a helping hand" New International Version (NIV). Women should be submissive to authority as long as the authoritarian is a person leading with excellence, honor and respect; then submission is to be warranted. In regards to submission in a marriage; the Bible states in Ephesians 5:22: "Wives, understand and support your husbands in ways that show your support for Christ. The husband provides leadership to his wife the way Christ does to his church, not by domineering but by cherishing. So just as the church SUBMITS to Christ as he exercises such leadership, WIVES should likewise SUBMIT to their husbands" New International Version (NIV). It goes on to say that Husbands are to show love to their wives like Christ does for the church. Submission is warranted to a man that falls under the authority of God; a woman is to submit to her husband with the regard that he is submitting to God. As a woman submits to her husband and confides in his leadership in the home and his wisdom in real life situations; God will honor her submission because he does not go back on his word. The woman that submits to her husband will see the fruits of her submission in the favor received from God and the peace in her home.

There are two real life situations that enlightened me in the appropriate way to act in a submissive demeanor. The first one was when I met Mr. Wisdom. I was in a low place in my life personally and spiritually. You see one of my closest friends just murdered his wife's lover and I felt guilty for not being able to stop him. In my mind since my friend called me the night before the murder numerous of times but I didn't feel like talking I didn't answer his call or call him back; so I believed I was at fault because I didn't answer the phone. LADIES!! We think that we can change the plans of FREE WILL. This is not the case; my friend had free will he was going to do what he had to do whether I picked up the phone or NOT! You see the Devil will lead you to believe that you have control over another human beings' actions, motives, words or behavior! So Not TRUE! Since I thought

I was GOD and I could've controlled my friend and I didn't; I decided to carry the luggage of guilt; the guilt was so heavy inside... I was feeling like a failure. I pride myself in being a reliable friend and so when that one day that I didn't answer the phone is the one day my good friend committed murder. What could I do but carry the guilt?! I felt as if I could've saved another human life. At this time, I knew that I needed God to renew my mind and to remove the guilt. I then remembered about a Church that I visited once; I remember getting good word from there. I decided to start going to that church and praying for an opportunity that the Holy Spirit would remove the burden I was carrying. When I first started going there the word was always exactly what I needed and carried me through a ton of bad times. The pastor at the time was going through a trial himself and the irony of God is that while he was going through his darkness his words was carrying me out my darkness into the light. After years of attending the church I become associates with Mr. Wisdom. You see I was pursuing my Undergrad in Religion and he was wise on many subjects and luckily for me Religion was one of them. I always looked at him in awe of how wise and down to earth he was. Since I was in the military, I ended up moving to Arizona but we kept in touch every once and a while. As time went on, I ended up separating from the Air Force and once I moved back to Texas we began to socialize on a frequent basis. The generosity and commitment that was instilled in Mr. Wisdom's veins was unmatchable. The man he was is one that I never witnessed or had an encounter with. He was a man of valor and a man that would communicate with you in a respectful manner. Sharing close moments and time together; I witnessed what it meant to be a patriarch of a family and the true meaning of submission: GOD's WAY! As a woman that grew up in a home where my voice always had to be louder than any other person in the room and I always had to state my opinion; in his presence I learned that was not TRUE! I had to learn to be silent and allow the wisdom in the room to speak and truly learn from who God put in my life to show me the true meaning of submission...according to the word! I had to retrain my way of thinking "that a man can't tell me what to do" I had to stop my brain patterns that tell me "no one tells me what to do"! I had to lay down my stubborn ways and mouth and truly ask God to allow me to see how to be submissive to a leader and God's vision for this leader. You see I had to trust God and his plan for this patriarch and to know that my work in this plan was for the kingdom! In this moment submission was a pleasure of mine and I became excited to serve! This season of submission in my life brought so much intelligence and humility to my spirit! My brain started to think outside the box I had envisioned for my life and provoked me to strive to be quiet while having a conversation instead of desperately waiting for me to interrupt and respond. God knew exactly where he had me and who was in my company to reveal to me my journey to become SUB to his MISSION for my life. While my time serving Mr. Wisdom my brother suddenly passed away. He was my younger brother 26 years old and a father to two beautiful children. He was my right hand man; we had plans to open up a yoga studio with a health café. He was finally in his own apartment and saved for a new car. He just won custody of his daughter and 4 days later he dies! I was thinking "This isn't supposed to happen GOD! He's younger than me! He just won custody of his daughter! Who will take care of her now!" the amount of confusion and questions I had for God were limitless but Mr. Wisdom had all the confidence "That in all things God works for the good of those who love him, who have been called to his purpose" 1 Thessalonians 5:18 New International Version (NIV) in that scripture I learned that I had to be SUB to the Mission of Christ for me, my brother and my niece. I had to understand that God is the beginning and the end and he knows what's for our good especially since my brother literally accepted God into his heart and home the day before he passed! In my heart I knew this was God's plan. I just had to submit to the fact that my brother was gone and I had to be ok with it! I had to renew my mind on the plans I had for my life that included my brother and submit to the mission God had for me and my life! I had to SURRENDER... EVERYTHING I ONCE KNEW! I had to submit my ways to God's ways and truly become a submissive WOMAN to my king, my father in Heaven. I decided to lay down my life for a second time and allow God to show me the way with helping my aunt with my niece and putting my selfish ways aside to give and fight for my niece in court. I had to accept that Junior my brother will no longer be on this earth; calling me for advice, laughing at my jokes, asking me to help him with his budget or sending me "Love you ANG" text messages. I had to submit to the fact that my niece no longer has a father on this earth! I had to step in and help direct her life. Now I was responsible on letting her know the amazing father she had! I had to submit to the fact that my nephew would NEVER remember his father and I had to step in and be the part of his father he can get to know as he gets older. I had to be the strong one to submit to God and honor his word to clean my brothers apartment after he passed and set up his funeral and smile my way through my pain. I had to submit to my God to make sure his mission on this earth for my family was accomplished! I for sure was going to do anything and everything my God created me for and if submitting my plans for God's purpose for my life was it… then I will be submitted on my way to HEAVEN!

<u>Knowledge Nugget:</u>

<u>It crushed me but I survived, I cried but I still SURVIVED! Through my Submission to God he imparted into me survival methods I never knew! You will survive too!</u>

Seven

REJECTION

Scripture: "As you come to him, the living Stone-REJECTED by humans but CHOSEN by God and precious to him..."
1 Peter 2:4 New International Version (NIV)

IT WAS A BEAUTIFUL SEASON in my life not only was it my favorite season "spring" but it was a season where I was finally at a place in my life that I was content in my singleness. I have come to terms with the death of my brother and the death of my relationship with Mr. Romantic. I have become comfortable in my skin to know that not having a boyfriend or husband was OK! I decided to start writing my book that God imparted upon me to write and I was practicing celibacy. I was finally over Mr. Smoothtalker and all his fictitious stories on his commitment to me and us "ONE DAY" being together. I have come to terms with the fact that Mr. Perfect will never mature enough and be courageous on us being in a relationship and I was OK with all of these broken hearted situations that I lived through! I would say I was confident in my position on being a single middle aged woman with no children but I was neglecting the fact that I had an enemy that studied me from the day I was born and he knew my behavior and desires more than I did! The enemy knew my purpose and would try every trick in the book to get me to derail off of the road to my destiny that God had for me. The fact was that I was actually too confident in my OWN strength instead of relying on GOD's STRENGTH AND GUIDANCE DAILY! During this season in my life that I fell asleep to the enemy's tricks he sent his last attempt to break me down.

One day as I was driving on base to work and I approached the gate guard my heart sank, my hands started trembling and my chest was pounding! I recognized this face that I deeply tried to bury long away in my memories, I recognized this laugh and sexy complexion and not to mention this military police uniform and the way it fitted his chest perfectly; oh yeah I remember this face this was the face that betrayed me to a level beyond comprehension, this was the man I fell in love with while my time on Augmentee duty at Las Vegas Air Base when I was in the national guard back in 2013! This was the man that I chose to forget and not deal with the lies, rejection and embarrassment that he put me through. You see while I was enjoying my life and thinking extremely highly of my progress and growth in overcoming heartbreak; the devil through an old demon in my path to knock me down and surly it worked. BUT GOD! What the devil meant for my harm God supernaturally turned around for my good!

You see; let me take you back; Mr. Attentive is his name. A man that was my type on the outside, listened and attended to all my needs. He understood my disabilities, he understood grief as we both lost grandparents that helped raise us but the icing on the cake; he was saved, attended church and LISTENED TO PRAISE AND WORSIP MUSIC! One of our favorites was "I give myself away" by William McDowell. I can remember us trading praise and worship songs like it was yesterday! I met him while I was in the National Guard serving as a Military Police Augmentee. We both had the same shift and days so we spent 12 hour days together. When you spend 12 hour days on a Gate checking ID cards TRUST ME you get to know someone real well; especially if your working overnights! Perfect situation for two young adults to fall in love when all you have is each other. LADIES!!!! READ THIS CAREFULLY! The devil knows where and how to trap you when he knows that you're getting ready to embark on the purpose God made you for. He will send counterfeits in your life to keep you from winning souls for the kingdom so you must ALWAYS STAY WOKE! The devil knew this time I wasn't going to fall for cheap talk and false realties so he sent a man that could connect with me spiritually and had a relationship with Christ! It worked but not for long; remember that God gives us free will and he will allow us to walk on the wrong path, get hurt and fall on our face but he will be there to bless our mess!

Mr. Attentive came along in the middle of two weeks of the painful bladder syndrome that I suffer from and with close to no sleep. Not to mention standing on my feet for hours on end in the cold winter nights! If you ever been to the desert during the winter nights you would know EXACTLY what I mean! There is no humidity just cold air and yes 30-degree weather in the winter months in Las Vegas! The devil knew when to send him during my weak state of mind and my body was physically depleted of energy. You see; Interstitial Cystitis also known as painful bladder syndrome can cause pelvic pressure along with frequency and an urgency to urinate continuously. At times this pain would not allow me to sleep or function like a normal human being. One of the overnights that I was in pain but working; Mr. Attentive brought me my favorite starbucks latte and vanilla bean scones! How did he know which scones were my favorite; I never shared that detail with him! He must've been watching me one day when I brought starbucks back from the Base Exchange. That warmed my heart that he was paying attention to the small details. Another day he brought in these warm patches that I could use for my lower abdomen to relax my bladder while we would stand outside at the gate. As we started sharing intimate details about our life we started to spend lunches and dinners together. During one of our meetings at the gym he slightly mentions that he's married but him and his wife are really not together and actually he wants a divorce and has asked his wife already! He went on to show me paperwork and new apartment leases. Now for me to take this all in was overwhelming! Like DUDE...really! But remember when I said the devil knows when to send you that COUNTERFEIT! Too bad I was so desperate for love and lonely in my singleness that I believed that he was truly getting a divorce and not engaging with his wife. I told him LOOK, I understand and I have been in the same situation before. I know it can take time to choose to separate then divorce and then to decide what will happen to his son. I told him to seek another persons advice or opinion. I agreed we would just be friends but as time went on and we grew closer we started or need I say… I caught feelings for him and he played an amazing ROLE in acting like he was deeply in love with me and I was his ultimate soulmate. I believed he was moving forward with the divorce because him and I always spent time together and he was never with his wife or was hiding anything. She didn't show up to the gate and when she would call him he would let me listen to the conversation and there was no love or likeness in their conversations; strictly business! You see but I should've stuck to what I have already learned; honoring the covenant of their marriage whether they were "together or not". Even though Mr. Attentive portrayed that he and his wife were headed towards divorce; I should've laid my boundary down and restricted him from spending time with me on a personal level… outside of work! That was my weakness; I believed him when he would tell me that he was going to move forward for us to be together and I also believed that he loved me unconditionally! That all came to an end…when his wife decided to pull up to my gate at 0 dark thirty with him in the car asking me what's the status of him and I? I can not explain to you the shock in my chest as this man SAT THERE AND SAID NOTHING! I pulled her aside and we talked on our own and I specifically told her; you need to talk to your husband cause your husband came for me and portrayed that you and him were not together! She proceeded to ask me the same question a million times until I finally said LOOK if you want to know what's going on or what went on with your husband and me we can talk but it will be another day cause I'm at work and today ain't the day! She said no just do me a favor don't contact my husband! I said AGAIN you need to tell your husband not me! It took me a whole 12 hour shift to gather my thoughts before I could go home. After my shift I sat in the corner of the office for 4 hours in shock; I tried to gather my thoughts and truly understand what just happened. I felt rejected beyond belief; confused with no rhyme or reason. As I put myself together, I thought to myself; next weekend were both back on the same shift and how are we going to work on the same GATE! I fell to my knees and balled my eyes out; pleading with God for forgiveness and strength!

Then the next weekend came and no Good Morning, no text messages between cars on the gates, no phonecalls at lunch, no pop up conversations at my post, no meetings at the track, no meetings at the security forces parking lot, no more helping me out with my car and no lunches at the bx or dinners on the Vegas Strip. Just like that... in a moment my life as I knew it changed just from a 10 min face to face conversation. I felt as if I was dropped in the middle of the ocean and didn't know if I could breathe any more on my own!! I felt like I was suffocating with no life line to grab on to. In that moment I had to stop all the thoughts or future plans with a man I thought was my future.

As I stand at my gate with one other co worker; Sgt Brown; in between us and he had no clue what was going on as Mr. Attentive acted normal so Sgt. Brown included us both in all jokes and extra curricular activities. Men don't catch on too quickly so he didn't realize a change in Mr. Attentive and I. Sgt. Brown didn't notice that our demeanor towards each other wasn't the same. I for sure wasn't going to tell anybody because this whole situation was HIGHLY embarrassing! As Mr. Attentive is laughing at Sgt. Brown's Jokes and leisurely talking about his wife and her birthday and what gift he got here... LADIES!!!! I'm STANDING RIGHT THERE! And this man that expressed a MILLION TIMES how much love he had for me; is talking about his wife and how amazing their night was at a Christmas party!

I started to think of the man that I fell in love with: a man that was 8 yrs old internally, a man that did not know how to handle his emotions or actions. I felt betrayed and rejection in a way I never felt before. I started to think of all the times he and I shared. The laughing, the serious talks, the plans we had for each other and I started to think to myself... I will never feel that affection again or experience those moments with the man I truly believed was my love. I had to come to realization that the chemistry was undeniable between us but our spirits didn't see eye to eye and they weren't in alignment to God's will. I couldn't stand there any longer and hear another word about his amazing date night with HIS WIFE! I paged my supervisor and asked him to cover me because of a "women's issue" he was always cool with me and I didn't have to explain much so MSgt Lopez came to my post to relieve me. I would go straight to the squadron bathroom and pray; in the upcoming month of us being on the same post the bathroom stall would became my best friend...my sanctuary that I would run to every time I felt tears welling up in my eyes or if I felt like slapping his head with my weapon. It was in this bathroom I would regroup my inner thoughts and start to reframe my words to match Gods word. As I starred at the bathroom ceiling and cried I would say:

God please give me the strength that surpasses all understanding. God please allow my brain to understand that the actions that Mr. Attentive gave was not love!!

God please remove the love in my heart for him and allow me to not feel a thing. Lord please fill my heart with your love.

I'm stronger then this… I can do this!

He does not care about you! He does not care about you!

He does not want you in his life! He does not care about you!

I repeated any one of these statements continuously until I stopped crying. Then I took a DEEP breath, cleaned my face and walked out like a champ. You got this!! You got this!!! I would position myself back on my post and say to myself you better not shed one tear in front of this lying, manipulative, immature man. Then I would start repeating Pslam 34:18 New International Version (NIV) "The Lord is close to the BROKEN HEARTED and SAVES those who are crushed in spirit." God's word is our weapons of mass destruction against the enemy. You need to understand the enemy will use these vulnerable opportunities of weakness to fill your brain with lies from the pit of hell! He will tell you to call an old boyfriend so you can feel better or sleep with an old boyfriend so you can feel loved again. Then once you do go back to what you once left; the devil will then bring condemnation on you. This becomes a vicious cycle that you don't realize until you seek daily guidance from God. I only had to endure this daily pain and aggravation for 8 weeks after the confrontation. My time on augmentee duty which was just 18 months was coming to an end and I was going back to the reenlistment office. The day finally came and I was back in my office; no more listening to his stories involving his wife or family. I smiled and thanked God for having my back along this mess that I did to myself. Yes the mess that I allowed to happen and allowed to stay involved in until I was confronted. I was a little upset that I wasn't seeing him anymore and he didn't make a way to talk to me. I was angry at him, he betrayed me, he lied to me, he played with my feelings, he abused my kindness, he had a whole wonderful family at home and I was alone… crying… heartbroken… tormented with the idea of him not really loving or caring about me at all! How did I have such bad judgement of character of a man; knowing I have experienced the worst of all kinds of men in my life and still in my mid 30's; I couldn't differentiate between fake and real love. Really?! I would imagine in my head a million times a day him walking in his front door and the whole family all happy daddy and mommy made it through! As I walked into a 500 sq.feet apartment with no welcoming party, no hugs or joys from anybody. Just me, the silence and a broken heart! I realized that at one point the man that looked into my eyes like I was his world would now look through me as if my presence did not exist.

Sometimes God is not going to change your situation he needs that situation to change your heart. It's in this moment that God had my attention my full attention! No distractions no running out with friends to ignore my broken heart! I decided I'm going to deal with this pain once and for all. I have escaped this for the last 18 years. It's now time. No TV no food no going out; I have to deal with me and being alone. I began to dive into the word everyday, I fasted and prayed for strength to be ok. When you're in a state of weakness you must fill your spirit with the word so it becomes natural for you to think of all the good God has for you. You see I was crying before work during work and after work. I just wanted to manage a single hour not losing my mind or fighting the thoughts of the times him and I spent together. I had to keep my composure! This is the goodness of God; I knew that God would shine bright like a diamond in my life and I knew that this incident wouldn't break me... it would actually mold me into the STRONG AND WORTHY WOMAN THAT GOD MADE ME TO BE. Even though I felt weak and defeated; God continued to pour revelation into my spirit. I thought I was free from Mr. Attentive's betrayal. I wasn't working with him on post and I was separating out of the Air National Guard and moving to Texas so I was good!

Until that one morning I pulled up to the gate on base on my way to work; 6 years later and BAM he's my gate guard checking my ID. I thought I was past him and over his betrayal until I looked in his eyes as he said Good Morning and once we locked eyes my heart wept and I literally said nothing to him and drove away. I was so upset, hurt, devasted, angry, dismayed and disappointed in myself! Why was I still moved by a man that played me 6 years ago! The sense of resentment that hid for a long time came up like a rushing volcano and I knew this feeling right here… this feeling was not of God and was not right. As I went to work in total disbelief; I felt weak and defeated. In my weakness God had the power to intertwine and interact with me. You see my depression made me think about my selfish needs. All I was thinking about was my feelings and my heart and how I could heal myself. You see I couldn't heal my heart only God could heal me! This is when I began setting up specific times to read daily affirmations on strength and overcoming disappointment. I also needed a new game plan to not see Mr. Attentive and not have to interact with him every day. I set up new routes to come to work because I refused to see his lying, manipulative, deceiving behind every morning! Long behold when you try to escape what your spirit needs to conquer so you can be a pillar in God's kingdom it won't be easy to avoid overcoming what hurt you. YOU HAVE TO FACE YOUR PAIN SO you can help others! As I would come in through the medical gate; long and behold Mr. Attentive was at the medical gate! As I would go to the BX for lunch so I wouldn't have to leave the base and take the risk on seeing him at the gate; Mr. Attentive was at the BX eating lunch as well! I could not get away from this guy and one day God whispered to my spirit; it's time… it's time to apologize to him for violating his marriage covenant! I said oh no not me! I didn't do anything wrong he LIED TO ME DAILY, BETRAYED MY TRUST and MANIPULATED ME TO BELIEVE HE WAS NOT WITH HIS WIFE! As I combated back and forth with this idea of me apologizing, I knew that I wanted to let go of the heaviness that lived inside me towards him. I decided to pray about me apologizing to him. After two weeks of prayer I began to feel that In order to get right with God I needed to forgive Mr. Attentive and ask for forgiveness as well; I was reminded of God's word in Mark 11:25 New International Version (NIV) "But when you are praying, first FORGIVE anyone you are holding a grudge against, so that your Father in heaven will forgive your sins too". I could no longer hold on to this resentment towards Mr. Attentive and then expect my father in heaven to forgive me of all the wrongs I have done. I had to come to the realization that I am not Perfect and I have hurt plenty of people in my life and God forgave me. Once I knew I would have to apologize so I can move forward in my life I decided to fast and pray for another week so God can show me when I should make my move. I was fearful of him rejecting my apology or him not responding in the way I wanted him to. LADIES! This is our problem; God told me to apologize…period! He didn't tell me to dissect the apology and the reaction I would receive! My duty was to apologize and move forward! I knew I couldn't do this on my own I started to pray for him, his wife and his family because I heard a message from Joyce Meyer stating "In order to get over a betrayal you must pray for them" this is what I did continuously; even though it was torture for his name and his wife's name coming out of my mouth as I would pray for peace and love between them… I still did it! Then one day… I was no longer mad and it was actually easy to pray for him and his wife. That's when I knew and I accepted God's suggestion to help my spirit man and I went all in. I sent the email and felt an insurmountable release of all the anger, resentment and disgust. I felt 1200 pounds being removed from my back! I felt released from all negativity connected to that betrayal situation back in 2013! I was FREE finally! He responded with a long apology and stated his head and heart still felt the same towards me but he was wrong and I deserved better! He wished me the best and said I'm sorry I thought I was ready but I can't leave right now! That's all I needed; an apology from his wrong doings and him accepting my apology. I was grateful!!!! I thought back to my days crying continuously and I was so grateful that he acknowledged my pain but I was even more grateful that God carried me to my healing journey. I had to endure that in my weakness I grew closer to God and his word! It reminded me of 2 Corinthians 12:9 New International Version (NIV) "But He said to me, "My grace is sufficient for you, for My power is perfected in weakness. Therefore, I will boast all the more gladly in my weaknesses, so that the power of Christ may rest on me." I realized during all this pain even when I believed I overcame all the pain on my own; God allowed an old wound to be resurrected so I could completely heal, finish this book and have to become dependent on God's word…not Man's love. In the middle of this great conflict; this is where God can do great miracles! And he did!

<u>Knowledge Nugget:</u>

<u>One Mistake in One Man made me into 1 whole WOMAN MIND, BODY and SOUL!</u>

Eight

INTIMACY

> **Scripture: "The LORD your God is in your midst, a mighty one who will save; he will rejoice over you with gladness; he will quiet you by his love; he will exult over you with loud singing." Zephaniah 3:17 New International Version (NIV)**

IN THE MIDDLE OF ALL these heartbreakes, God was waiting for me with open arms! No judgement, ridicule, disgust, rejection, neglect, sarcasm or reprisal….. just UNCONDITIONAL LOVE! A love that I have never physically experienced, a love that is an agape love. Agape means unconditional love: a love for someone without expecting anything in return. A love that was never taught to me or displayed to me in real life. My parents taught me the level of love that they endured themselves; they could not have given me something they did not have for themselves. It's like asking your friend to borrow a million dollars and she works for an $8.00 dollars an hour job and is barely paying her rent; there's no way she can pull a million dollars out of nothing. It's the same difference! Someone cannot give you what they do not have! You see; I was ignorant to the fact that my many heartbreaks, stubbornness behavior, disobedient and disrespectful ways as a wife and child of God was not a normal way of living or behaving. I allowed the enemy to keep me bound to my past. I didn't have the tools to overcome the negativity of my upbringing. I didn't know that I had to take God's word which is the truth and prophesy the words over my life daily. As a kid I didn't know any better and in my times of despair; God was carrying me. God carried me through the night terrors of hearing my mother get beat or her beat on any one of her husbands. God was there when I had to run into a closet with my little brother and sister because of the domestic violence. God was there when I had to run to a neighbor's house to call my aunt because of the domestic violence. God was there when a few men kidnapped me simply because a family friend owed them money. God was there when I had no one to talk to at night about the fear in my heart of me having no where to stay. God was there when I got extremely ill and I would have to stay in the hospital at night by myself because everyone had to go to work in the morning so they would leave me in the hospital to fend for myself. God was there when my mother and grandmother would have a fist fight and I would have to go with my grandmother to the ER and sit there while the Doctor asked my grandmother "What Dog bit you?" as she would have to say with much embarrassment…"My daughter". God was there in the ER room sitting next to me, giving me strength to endure the drama with my upbringing. God was there by blessing me with amazing aunts, uncles and my grandmother. Through it all GOD WAS THERE!

After 37 years of trying to figure out love, life and laughter I first had to understand my generations dysfunction; in regards to love or the lack there of. I had to depict the lack of love my parents had and then I was able to recognize their reasoning on their role of not displaying love in my life. I also had to understand the love my grandmother and aunt displayed so I could then recognize that their love was rigid but it was limitless! Once my mentality understood the lack of love my parents, grandmother and aunts received; I than started to reflect deeply on who I was, what I liked, my personality and my behavior towards love. It was in this time in my life; in the middle of my many broken hearts that I decided to release the abandonment, embrace the rejection, dig deep into my soul and date myself. It's after this time I decided to invest in myself and my purpose on who God made me to be on this Earth. I also needed to make time for intimacy with my God that created me. I needed to know God in an intimate way with no men clouding my vision or robbing my time away from my God! It was finally time to stand up and have a voice for my true desires! I decided to relinquish my control over every detail of my life and give my whole life to the ever knowing and everlasting God!

I surrendered to God and his will and decided to let him control every area of insecurity and vulnerability that hid along with all the pain that I learned to run away from. I then opened my soul to release all the brokenness and devastation of the constant disappointments that I allowed to develop me into a dysfunctional woman; I was. The unleashing of my pain birthed a new level of me that was created by God and him alone. The mishaps, unfortunate failures, divorces, break ups, abortion, sickness in my body and abandonment…. Was used by God. He used all of my brokenness to catapult me into a whole mature woman. And for that I'm grateful!

I will end with this: during my many years of heart break, rejection and disappointment from my relationships that I allowed! I finally decided to invest in myself; Spiritually, Physically and Emotionally. I knew I had to figure out a way to renew my mind so I strategically came up with a healing plan for my everyday life. I read a famous Poem titled "Phenomenal Women" by Maya Angelou, Scriptures on Love and Healing; EVERYDAY! The poem helped me gain my worth, self-value and confidence in me as a woman. These encouraging rituals of reading the poem and scriptures everyday slowly but surely set me free! Till today I still have these same rituals! You have to feed your mind daily on information that feeds your inner soul and recreates the neurons in your brain that control your mood. I've been doing this for so many years that If I'm out of town I will wake up earlier than anyone I'm with and lock myself in the bathroom and read my scriptures, poems or affirmations for the day! In the end you must put GOD and YOURSELF FIRST then you are able to "FIND YOUR WORTH IN THE MIDDLE OF A BROKEN HEART!"

Knowledge Nugget:

Be accountable in your actions vertically; meaning you only are responsible for respecting and honoring our God above! You don't do for the people that are horizontal from you but you do for the Savior that is Vertical from you!

Before your close the book... please pay attention to the next part!

IF YOU FEEL THAT YOU are all alone while your raising your children by yourself, having dinner by yourself, going to the movies by yourself, paying for health insurance by yourself, experiencing pain by yourself and managing the stressors of life by yourself... YOUR NOT BY YOURSELF! You have God, Jesus Christ and the HOLY SPIRIT that yearns to be a part of your everyday LIFE! All you have to do is accept Jesus Christ into your life as your Lord and Savior and trust me he will handle the rest. Right now, read the scripture below and repeat the statement that follows:

This scripture is from the book of Romans 10: 9-11 New International Version (NIV)

"If you declare with your mouth, Jesus is Lord, and BELIEVE in your heart that God raised him from the dead, you will be saved. For it is with your heart that you believe and are justified, and it is with your mouth that you profess your faith and are saved."

LORD FATHER GOD, I ask you to come to me today as I confess to you all my sins, all my evil intentions, all my sarcastic remarks, all my doubt in your capabilities, all my doubtful thoughts, all my disobedience to your word and your people! I ask that Jesus Christ come into my life as my Lord and Savior! I believe in my heart that he was crucified and killed for my sins for my salvation! I ask that you receive my apology and show me favor with your forgiveness for my old ways of being and old ways of thinking! I accept your son and the Holy Spirit into my life and heart in Jesus Name I DECREE AND DECLARE and it is DONE! AMEN!

NO LONGER ARE YOU WALKING ON THIS EARTH ALONE! Get yourself a good Bible that you can read and get into an intimate relationship with your savior! He will blow your socks off and the Holy Spirit will give you peace beyond comprehension!

My to go to dating lists

The lists that follow are from a suggestion that the beautiful, talented and selfless Christian Entrepreneur was given to me. Ms. Dana Channel suggested I create lists to help my fellow ladies with an idea of what women should look for in their spouse and who they should strive to be before they put themselves out in the dating scene. These are the characteristics that I worked hard to become. These are also the characteristics that I look for in a spouse. Remember you attract what you are!

Goals to achieve while becoming a Whole Woman of God:

1. Know who God is and his word
2. Know your Value and Worth as a Woman
3. Dedicate time for your body to get rest and healing
4. Study yourself and your inner desires
5. Focus on your PURPOSE
6. Learn to submit to the word, leadership and your husband
7. Find time to help other women build up their dreams or goals
8. Live authentically
9. No praises are needed from everyone or anyone to feel valuable
10. Failure is not a failure but an opportunity to learn

What a Whole Women seeks in a Spouse:

1. Have they received Jesus Christ into their heart as their Lord and Savior?
2. Can they pray for you?
3. Do they attend Church and Tithe?
4. Are they committed to God as much as you are?
5. Do they know their own Purpose?
6. Are they working everyday towards their Purpose?
7. What values do they bring to your relationship?
8. How do they handle their finances?
9. How do they treat their immediate family members?
10. How do they handle stress?

I want to send an air hug to you for taking the time with me and reading about my journey! I pray it will give you a sense of peace, belonging and hope! Much Love... Valentina Richardson